SURREALISM:

Theater, Arts, Ideas

SURREALISM

Theater, Arts, Ideas

by Nahma Sandrow

Harper & Row, Publishers
New York, Evanston, San Francisco, London

STANDARD BOOK NUMBER: 06-136075-9

Library of Congress Catalog Card Number: 77-159629

CONTENTS

PREFACE

The Surrealist movement, which developed out of Dada shortly after World War One, has interest for us even beyond the art work produced by its official members. As the first strong statement of certain tendencies dominant in the arts of our own day—in particular, the perception of and enthusiastic commitment to non-rationality and the redefinition of the roles of artist and audience—the Surrealist movement deserves, and is currently beginning to receive, attention and respect.

Studies of the Surrealist movement have been appearing for forty-five years, beginning with André Breton's *First Surrealist Manifesto* in 1924; a partial list appears in the bibliography of this book. Curiously enough, very few of these have dealt with the movement's contributions to the theater. And of these few, not one that I know of has addressed itself directly to the relationship between the principles and general practice of the movement and the specific characteristics of the drama which the movement produced. This neglect is particularly striking in view of the theatrical and cinematic nature of surrealism as a whole. I have tried to remedy it.

Precisely because with the Surrealist movement new tendencies emerged which have since been importantly assimilated into Western cultural and intellectual life, the word "surrealism" creates problems of definition. The neologism was originally coined by Guillaume Apollinaire in his program notes to the ballet *Parade* in 1917. Now the "current accepted usage" of the term has been loosened to designate something "crazy, dreamlike, and funny,"[1] or a wide range of art works or, even more broadly, "a mode of sensibility which cuts across all the arts in the twentieth century."[2] In Martin Esslin's *The Theater of the Absurd*, dramatists as dissimilar as Brecht, Lorca, Fitzgerald, and cummings—none of whom subscribed to the surrealist ideal—are all included with Apollinaire and Aragon in a chapter section about surrealism.[3] However, I prefer to restrict my use of the word to that which pertains to the official Surrealist movement: the movement's members and their work, and the movement's formal principles. Such limitations actually free us to see the movement as a specific historical phenomenon, inseparable from the environment which produced it, which has extended into modern thought in certain ways.

In line with this intention to concentrate upon the Surrealist movement in its restricted historical context, we will examine the movement's activities in Paris only, the city of its birth, even though in the course of this half-century, surrealist art manifestations have occurred as far from Paris as Russia, Japan, and South America. And we will be primarily concerned with the years of the movement's early development and full bloom: approximately the second and third decades of this century.

The Preface is the place to get straight the difference between surrealism and German expressionism. Similarities of period, mood, political tendencies, and world view have occasionally led historians to confuse the two. However there are major distinctions to be made between them. Obviously expressionism was primarily German and surrealism was primarily French. But a much more important difference is that whereas expressionism displayed a strong tendency toward abstractness in art, surrealism

---

1. Maurice Nadeau, *The History of Surrealism*, translated by Richard Howard, p. 9.
2. Susan Sontag, *Against Interpretation*, p. 269.
3. Martin Esslin, *The Theater of the Absurd*, chapter VI.

consistently rejected the abstract in favor of the concrete. Another basic difference lies in the attitudes of the two movements toward the subconscious. Both explored the subconscious; but the expressionists preferred to remain absolutely rational: to manipulate nonrationality, deliberately creating works to express a semblance of nonrationality, which spectators, equally rational, were then invited to see. The surrealists, on the other hand, were committed to nonrationality as an ideal in all their actions, including creation. Closely related is the difference in aesthetic theory between the two movements: the Expressionists preserved the traditional relationship of artist and audience, while the Surrealists developed something quite new: an art work which existed only as an expression of the artist's identity and through which the audience could share the artist's role.

There are two appendices: *Free Entry* (*Entrée Libre*), the only English translation of Roger Vitrac's newly discovered dream play; and a list of the surrealist plays mentioned in the text, with information about their publication and original productions.

I would like to thank several people for their very kind help and advice: Howard Stein of the Yale Drama School, Stanley Kauffmann, David S. Meranze, Philip Eidelberg, Susan Yankowitz, Marthe Eidelberg. I am particularly grateful to Annabelle Henkin of Tel Aviv University for guiding me to several rare photographs of surrealist theatrical performances. This book is dedicated to Philip and my parents.

SURREALISM:

Theater, Arts, Ideas

CHAPTER ONE

The Historical Background of Surrealism

The most conspicuous sight in Paris today is the Eiffel Tower, which still strikes the eye as freshly and unavoidably as it did in 1889, when it was erected as part of the Paris Exposition of that year, the centennial of the French Revolution. Beginning in 1887, when plans for its construction were announced, Parisian attitudes crystallized, from passionate partisans of the Tower to equally passionate opponents. Since the Eiffel Tower was designed to assert France's participation and even leadership in the contemporary technological progress, and since it was at the same time virtually the only single conspicuous evidence of that leadership—and since, further, the Tower was able to serve as catalyst, arousing emotions so violent that they can be explained only as expressions of attitudes toward forces which the Tower represented—for all these reasons, an examination of contemporary attitudes toward the Eiffel Tower becomes a reflection of contemporary attitudes toward technology as a whole. By restricting ourselves to the one symbol, we may achieve a broad general perspective: a view of early twentieth-century Paris comparable to that enjoyed by the throngs who climbed 1,051 feet to the top of the Tower in order to look down. This was the Paris which produced the surrealists and their audience.

These attitudes toward the Tower seemed to occur in two waves: first, the original reactions strongly for and against the

Tower; and later the Dada-surrealist view, which was notably affectionate toward the Tower but for a totally new set of reasons and in a way possible only for a generation that had never known a Paris without an Eiffel Tower.

In 1887 the Exposition Committee, headed by a M. Alphand and by M. Edouard Lockroy (Minister of Commerce and Industry), chose Gustave Eiffel's project to serve as one gateway to the rectangular Exposition grounds. They chose the project because it was a supreme technological achievement; and although it would serve varied purposes, it would serve them all through modern technological means. At 1,051 feet in height, the Tower was the highest structure in the history of the world, inconceivable in any previous era.[1] Eiffel himself was a new phenomenon, not an architect at all, but an engineer. His use not of stone but of an iron skeleton, and then his refusal to mask the skeleton with a stone façade for conventional beauty, enabled the Tower to rise to great heights without a commensurate gain in weight. Thus a comparatively small base provided sufficient support to balance those 1,051 feet in height. The open iron lacework which replaced solid walls allowed the winds to pass through the Tower so that, meeting no resistance, they did not threaten to topple the structure.

For all its functions, both pleasure-giving and strictly utilitarian, the Tower depended on its technological innovations. Simply being an unprecedented distance up in the air was a considerable amusement for visitors to the Exposition; the Tower also provided modern restaurants on various levels, complete with special garbage-disposal chutes, and modern elevators for reaching them. As a station for scientific experiments, especially meteorological, as a center for telephone, telegraph, and eventu-

---

1. Similar projects had been advanced in England in 1833 and in Philadelphia in 1874, but neither of these was actually attempted.

ally radio communications, and as the world's biggest lightning conductor, its potential services were impressive, although they remained, on the whole, only potential.

When Eiffel told an interviewer that his ambition had been to erect "an Arch of Triumph for the Industrial Age,"[2] and when he spoke of his pride, and of the right of all France to share in that pride, he was in a sense speaking for his generation. Scientific man had triumphed, and the Tower was both scientific instrument and monument to science.

The Tower edifice had been envisaged originally as temporary. No mention seems to have been made of the value of the Tower to posterity. The implication was that future generations would eventually outdistance this achievement as it had outdistanced the past. Thus the Tower's beauty was a temporary by-product of its existence, and permanence was not a consideration. Change itself was among the modern virtues that the Tower celebrated.

But naturally not everyone in Paris was prepared to accept such widespread change. In order to appreciate the meaning of the "Tower fever"[3] which swept the majority of Paris, we ought to see who reserved their loyalty for the original Arch of Triumph and for Notre Dame, and why. Invoking with relish the story of Babel, the Tower's enemies first predicted that the Tower would never rise. Then they began to petition, denouncing the ongoing construction.[4] The Tower would ruin the beauty of the city, destroy the sense of history created by the old buildings and monuments, throw off the gridiron pattern of the boulevards laid out

2. Jean Prévost, *Eiffel*, p. 41.
3. François Poncetton, "La Tour Eiffel a cinquante ans, I," *La Revue universelle*, p. 27.
4. The most famous and most virulent of these petitions came out on February 1, 1887. (For a full reprint, see Prévost, *Eiffel*, pp. 38–40.) It is interesting that among the signers—all of whom were elderly men and dead within fifteen years—were two playwrights, Victorien Sardou and Alexandre Dumas fils, who used the conventional rigid "well-made play" form to express an, on the whole, equally conservative commitment to nineteenth-century social conditions.

by Haussmann between 1850 and 1870 (and itself denounced at that time for ruining Paris), and dwarf the dignity of the famous public buildings and cathedrals. That the Tower could enhance the Paris scene—or even be assimilated into the city's architecture—was inconceivable to these critics, who wished to defend Paris from the inroads of technology.

But the "beauty of the city," as exemplified by Notre Dame, and the "sense of history" and even the "dignity" of Paris were no longer such inarguable values. The beauty of the "laws of force"[5] was the only beauty that Eiffel claimed for his Tower, and for him and his champions that was sufficient. Continuing change was more desirable than a consciousness of the past. And the Church, whose dignified tradition was incorporated in Notre Dame, was beginning to seem irrelevant in the face of scientific discoveries, sixty years after Renan's *Life of Christ.*

Most of Paris, far from trying to hold back the approach of the Eiffel Tower and of what the petitioners called the "mercantile imaginations"[6] of the twentieth century were, on the contrary, embracing the new era with joy. In Western Europe as a whole— and in America, which makes understandable the popular contemporaneous French craze for all things American—life was conspicuously changed by the industrial technological revolution.

It is true that France was always slow to industrialize; the Eiffel Tower indeed remained fairly isolated in Paris, never flanked by skyscrapers, almost the only such achievement of its period, unlike, for example, the Haussmann city plan, which developed during the industrially dynamic pre-World War One period. France's postwar failure to develop, as compared with England and Germany, is usually attributed to her meager resources in coal and manpower.[7] However, we may conjecture

---

5. Prévost, *Eiffel*, p. 41.
6. Ibid., p. 39.
7. See, John Clapham, *Economic Development of France and Germany 1815–1914.*

that this makes it easier for us to separate the material transformation which accompanied it. It also helps explain the Surrealist attitude toward industrialization.

In late nineteenth-century France, machines were able to turn out vast quantities of mass-produced things. Advertising to encourage mass consumption expanded into a big business among many large businesses. The telephone and telegraph, the radio and phonograph and cinema, the automobile and airplane—all these had been recently invented, or at least were only recently in widespread use. Communications became faster and more thorough than had ever seemed possible.

Technology glorified and influenced the age, and the age gloried in it. Art reflected this, and it became the basis for new ways of thinking about art. The Italian Futurist painters, for example, began in 1908 to derive their primary themes and motifs from a celebration of the machine and rapid mechanical motion.[8] Dufy, Utrillo, Delaunay, and Henri Rousseau included the Eiffel Tower prominently in their Paris landscapes.[9] Marcel Duchamp, before he affiliated himself with the surrealists, began to make loving studies of a chocolate grinder he'd passed in a Rouen shop window.[10] Apollinaire wrote love lyrics to technology like this stanza.

> Paris evenings drunk on gin
> Flaming with electricity
> The trolley cars green lights on their spines

8. For example, Severini's *Nord-Sud* (*Métro*) (1913), and Carra's *What the Streetcar Said to Me* (1913), both in private collections in Milan. (Nord-Sud, the métro line between Montparnasse and Montmartre, was in 1917 to be the name of a proto-surrealist periodical).

9. Utrillo: *Rue Saint-Dominique à Paris* (1911), in a private collection in Paris; Delaunay: *Tour Eiffel aux Arbres* (1910) and *Tour Eiffel* (1910), both in the Solomon R. Guggenheim Foundation in New York; Dufy: *Paris* (n.d.), in a private collection in Paris; Rousseau: *Moi-Même, Portrait-Paysage* (1890), in the National Gallery of Prague.

10. From the original *Chocolate Grinder No. 1* (1913), he developed variations up to *The Bride Stripped Bare by Her Bachelors, Even* (*The Large Glass*) (1915–1925), now in New York's Museum of Modern Art.

> Play along the staves of tracks
> The music of their machine madness[11]

New art media were emerging: photography, the moving picture, the phonograph. From the late 1860s, poster advertisements by Grasset, Chéret, Toulouse-Lautrec and others exulted in their own up-to-date brassiness. High-power advertising through graphic arts, vulgar slogans, and especially neon lighting was part of the scene in its own right and served both as art and as natural environment. Apollinaire observed that science was beginning to "liberate [reality] from its assumed synonymity with the natural."[12] Artifacts of daily life, such as recognizable bits of advertisements and slogans, turned up in collages and poetry.[13] Folk-song motifs had been for a long time already woven through symphonic music, but the effect of these new inclusions was to enhance the impression of newness rather than to refer back to the tradition, and to lessen the distinction between the art work and the world outside.

In the theater, André Antoine founded his Théâtre Libre in Paris in 1887 in order to reproduce onstage the industrialized world outside. Zola (*Thérèse Raquin*), Becque (*The Vultures*) the early Hauptmann (*The Weavers*), Galsworthy (*Strife*)— they all attempted, by examining "slices of life" ("tranches de

11.   . . .
> Soirs de Paris ivres de gin
> Flambant de l'électricité
> Les tramways feux verts sur l'échine
> Musiquent au long des portées
> De rails leur folie de machines
                    . . .

Apollinaire, "La Chanson du Mal-Aimé" in *Alcools* in *Oeuvres Poétiques*, p. 59.
12. Anna Elizabeth Balakian paraphrasing Apollinaire's words in *Surrealism. The Road to the Absolute*, p. 55.
13. For example, Raoul Haussmann's collage *Head* (1923) and Hanna Hoch's collage *Cut with the Kitchen Knife* (1919), both in Hamburg. Also Apollinaire's collage-poem "Les Femmes" in *Alcools* (1913), *Oeuvres Poétiques*, p. 123.

vie"), to deal with the changed Europe. Those playwrights who turned their backs on contemporary culture—Maeterlinck (*The Intruder*), Yeats (*At the Hawk's Well*), Rostand (*Chantecler*)— did escape the atmosphere of aggressive industrialization, but not the impulse to construct their fantasies with the machine's perfect internal logic.

Thus developments in the arts are evidence that, to the generation which built it and welcomed it, the Tower was a beloved symbol of themselves; it seemed to them quite simply "ours."[14] To some members of this generation, especially the older members, it seemed undeniably representative of the age, but repellent for that very reason.

Meanwhile the Tower was changing its role as time passed. A new generation was emerging: young people who had never known a Paris without the Tower. This generation included our Dadaists and Surrealists. For them the dichotomy of reality vs. fantasy, each extreme with its own equivalent logic, was losing its meaning. The traditional beauty of Notre Dame meant no more to them than did the institutions, national and religious, which built the cathedral. And the Tower's revolutionary nature was also largely lost for them. The Tower's charms were of another sort entirely.

For this attitude, too, developments in the arts provide our evidence. In 1913, Guillaume Apollinaire, whom André Breton was to call the "patron saint of surrealism"—one of whose particular gifts was an instinct for the cultural trends of the future— signaled a whole new way of looking at the Tower and at the age. In the first lines of "Zone," the poem he and his disciples considered the battle cry of the younger generation, he saluted the Tower:

14. "à nous," François Poncetton in "La Tour Eiffel a cinquante ans, II," *La Revue universelle*, p. 23.

> At last you are tired of that bygone world
> Shepherdess O Eiffel Tower the flock of bridges
> bleats this morning[15]

Thus the Tower was no longer solely a triumph of rationality, though it retained its role as defier of tradition ("tired of that bygone world"). The Tower has taken on another, simultaneous aspect: a shepherdess. The Tower's material identity connects it with its bridges-sheep. This fancy does not try to rise above the Tower's iron reality but rather to play with that reality and view it from a fresh perspective, revealing a new and lively charm. This double and shifting perspective was to be typical of surrealism.

That the pastoral image in "Zone" functions further as a slyly mocking counterpoint to the poem's grimly urban atmosphere is equally part of the poet's intention. The incongruity, implying a certain irreverence toward the modern deities of technological progress as well as toward the traditional artistic figures, was also to be a favorite surrealist tone.

We are looking at the surrealists' attitude toward technology because they expressed in particularly lively—or compulsive—fashion a new way of thinking which was quickly gaining strength. Twenty years before World War One heresy lay in vaunting technology over tradition: in preferring the Eiffel Tower, for example, to Notre Dame. Now these members of the younger generation were committing an equal heresy by refusing to be respectful to the fruits of human reason.

After all, it had become obvious by now that unlike what the Haussmann boulevards had been, the Tower was not part of a

---

15. À la fin tu es las de ce monde ancien
   Bergère ô tour Eiffel le troupeau des ponts bêle ce matin

   . . .
   "Zone" in *Alcools, Oeuvres Poétiques*, p. 39.
   Ten years later Yvan Goll was to write in a poem called "Paris Brûle" ("Paris Burns"): ". . . an electric animal circus turns/around your metal geyser/Eiffel Tower . . ."

dynamic, politically powerful France; it was not a continuation of a wave of construction of which the boulevards had been an early product; rather, it was a monument to a technology which was building very little, and to a France overpowered twice in fifty years. The irony of the Exposition for which the Tower was built now began to surface: the Exposition honored the future by commemorating the past: the French Revolution. And an extra absurdity lay in the fact that the Revolution itself further retarded possible industrialization by splitting and rigidifying social classes. Besides, the Tower was almost useless. How then could intelligent people look up (except literally) to the Tower?

Attitudes were changing, and the way the surrealists dealt with the Tower is a clue. This young group adopted the Eiffel Tower not as a symbol of dynamic technology but as a technological pet. They painted pictures of the Tower for the fun of it—and for the fun of being heretical. Indeed the very fact that the Tower had begun by affronting conservatives further endeared it to the surrealists, who were pleased to carry on the precedent by affronting their own now-conservative contemporaries by their unorthodox reactions. The Tower was a monumental rude gesture.

Even the way that the surrealists incorporated the Tower in their art works shows their irreverence. In 1921, Jean Cocteau wrote an entertainment called *The Wedding on the Eiffel Tower* (*Les Mariés de la Tour Eiffel*). A wedding party, held for no particular reason in a restaurant on the Eiffel Tower, abounds in absurd surprises. Narrated by two phonographs and rich in telegrams, photographs, trains, and other products of technology, the play derives its frolicsome tone from its refusal to take these products seriously. For example, the following dialogue occurs in the play without warning or explanation:

GRANDFATHER: . . . What does my grandson want?
CHILD: I want someone to buy me some bread to feed the Eiffel Tower.
GRANDFATHER: They sell it down below. I'm not going down.

CHILD: I want to feed the Eiffel Tower.
GRANDFATHER: It is only fed at certain hours. That's why it has
  grilles around it.
CHILD: I want to feed the Eiffel Tower.

In the play, products of technology have been reduced to pets or
favorite toys and furthermore possess lovable human foibles: for
example, the camera tries to produce a "birdie" but keeps getting
confused and produces lions and bathing beauties instead. The
plot, a mélange of music and dance, deliberately defies all logic
of incident or construction. It's all absurd.

  The absurd aspect of everything traditionally respected was in
fact a dominant note of the young artists of the day, the spokes-
men of their generation. The surrealists in particular took upon
themselves the expression of this absurdity. In the art of surrealists and their contemporaries, from Apollinaire's first lyrical
glimpsing of the shepherdess in the Tower to Cocteau's playful
possession of the Tower for an evening of artful silliness, we can
see a number of contemporary manifestations of a similar rebellion against reason, a visceral perception that reason was irrelevant to current conditions—a refusal to take reason seriously, as
is particularly essential to the French cultural tradition, or to
respect anyone who did so.

  This rebellion had been seething for a long time; retreat into
fantasy had been a partial release of the impulse. But the war
exploded the rebellion into full consciousness. World War One
applied technology, devising new weapons such as poison gas and
an early form of airplane bombers. However, the war's results,
especially in the opinion of the young men who were forced to do
the actual fighting, were the opposite of rational: battlefield
horrors and a shaken Europe. And, as an extra joke on France's
national pride, her victory had felt almost as bitter as defeat.

  The experience proved traumatic for many of these young
men, permanently embittered against the ideals and society which

had created the war. Jacques Vaché, André Breton, Louis Aragon, Alain Salmon—these, and many other members or associates of Dada and surrealism became strongly pacifist. George Grosz, for example, was a German contemporary whose savage cartoon *Fit for Active Service* (1916) shows army officers and doctors with happy piggish faces approving the examination of a live skeleton. Angry violence became one of their predominant moods and, in particular, "épater le bourgeois"—whom they held responsible for the war and indeed for maintaining all the values of the establishment—was a goal they never lost sight of. (France has a tradition of strong antibourgeois feelings and sudden and violent reversals: one evidence of both tendencies is the popularity of more-or-less formal anarchy for almost the last two centuries, quite independently of Communist and Socialist party policies.)

But the war only brought to consciousness the phenomenon of changing ideas which already existed before the war. "A political counterpart" to contemporary "social upheavals,"[16] the war shocked its participants into consciousness that trends of thought which were ostensibly and in intention applications of rigorous technological reasoning to physical fact, were actually tending instead to lead away into realms which ultimately evaded reasoning. These trends of thought involved ideas about reasoning such as philosophy and psychology.

The thinker who most directly influenced the surrealists along these lines was Sigmund Freud, although, as we shall see, other fields of science and of abstract thought also affected them. Freud published *The Interpretation of Dreams* in 1900 and *Wit and Its Relation to the Unconscious* in 1920. According to popular understanding of his lectures and writings, their thrust was to discredit man's conscious intellect by revealing its subservience to the violence of his hidden chaotic desires. The Eiffel Tower, rising

16. Walter H. Sokel, *The Writer in Extremis*, p. 1.

suddenly from the Champ-de-Mars amid the neat boulevards, was, of course, a classic Freudian symbol. Ironically, what had begun as an attempt to apply clearheaded scientific investigation to the human soul seemed to become evidence that the soul—or psyche—defied science by ultimately retaining its mystery.

Man's dreams and reveries of freely associated images thus seemed of more significance than his intellectual formulations in revealing his true nature; even dreams seemed to possess a certain inexplicable creative energy of their own. The traditional conception of man in the image of a rational god, threatened by Darwin, was irreparably damaged. Bourgeois social institutions predicated on such a concept were perhaps untenable. An implication was that social order does not express man's nature but merely represses it. A further possible inference, already drawn by Rousseau, was that all order is inimical to the true nature of man.

By 1915, when André Breton, a former medical student, was serving in an army hospital for the mentally ill in St. Dizier, Freudian methods were familiar even in France, one of the last Western European countries to accept them fully. Freud and Breton met once and carried on a limited correspondence in the 1920s. However, Freud was to complain to Breton of France's continued resistance to his ideas some years later. (We may speculate that just as France's resistance to the full assimilation of industrialization enabled the surrealists to retain consciousness of industrialization as an isolated phenomenon and thus to react to it powerfully, so France's resistance to modern psychiatry also allowed the surrealists to espouse it with single-minded force.)

Another contemporary gesture beyond rationality, closely linked to psychoanalysis, was the emergent interest in physical and especially cultural anthropology. Elemental man was discovered beneath his façade of discipline and logic, as the Tower revealed itself without decoration; primitive society offered a fascinating glimpse of man in a state of nature. The cult of the innocence of childhood revived, though the definition of innocence had changed. Similarly, in an attempt to find the threatening truth rather than a romanticized Rousseau-ean noble savage, Kroeber, Malinowski, and others wrote early texts in anthropology. Artifacts of primitive life became the rage in Paris around 1907.[17] Artists like Picasso experimented with masks and carvings. African music, often savored indirectly through American jazz, was also extremely popular.[18]

Here again the attempt to analyze social systems so as to extract certain mechanical laws was unexpectedly yielding an exciting sense of mysterious primitive forces. Rituals and myths, examined intellectually, proved to have power to an inexplicable degree over the most civilized of Parisians and to be connected in imagery with dreams still universally dreamed.

Parallel expressions of loss of faith in logic and intellection were to be found in more abstract studies as well. In 1915 Albert Einstein's researches in physics led him to publish his General Theory of Relativity, which was popularly interpreted as an admission of the limitations of rationality: ". . . the real world isn't what we thought, the best-founded conceptions . . . they're false. False our old conceptions of space, false the time we've fabricated."[19] "The diffusion of Einstein's ideas prepared the postwar generation psychologically to accept the most disconcerting hypotheses, to explore the ever growing domain of the unknown. . . . [It] disintegrated common sense (all that was left of former

---

17. In 1917, a collection of Oceanic art, for example, inspired a pamphlet called *Le musée vivant* to which a number of people contributed appreciations: *L'Art Océanien* (Paris, chez Paul Guillaume, 1917).

18. Dada actually organized "des *soirées nègres* de danse et de musique improvisées" which signified to them a rediscovery, "dans les profondeurs de la conscience, les sources exaltantes de la fonction poétique." (Paris: Association populaire des amis des musées).

19. Nadeau, *History of Surrealism*, p. 48.

confidence in rationality)."[20] Of course the ironic fact was that Newton's laws had not been threatened, as far as they went; the terror, if terror there was, lay in the realization that things were moving so fast that they needed a whole new set of laws to explain them—laws which were as invisible to common sense as molecular activities were to the naked eye.

Nineteenth-century philosophers, such as Kant and Hegel, had already questioned "our best-founded conceptions" of "the real world." The philosopher with whose work the surrealists were best acquainted was a young lecturer very popular at that time (1900–1921) at the Collège de France in Paris. Henri Bergson's writings resemble official surrealist statements of principles. He valued intuition above intellection; he tried to experience time duration condensed by sensed simultaneity; he described matter in terms of an intuited *élan vital.*

Marcel Proust's novel *Remembrance of Things Past,* written mostly in the second decade of the century, reflects these concepts which were the context of the development of surrealism. Proust assimilated into the novel's form and content his perceptions of the relativity of time, of the illusory nature of rational thought, and of the mysterious workings of the subconscious. He also dealt with the disintegration of established social institutions in the face of technology and war. As psychiatric and other research made all rationally acquired knowledge seem increasingly questionable, Proust's withdrawal into an investigation purely of and through his own psyche had an integrity which resembled the surrealists' own revolutionary stance; unlike his younger contemporaries, however, Proust retained a commitment to French cultural tradition.

Bergson, who was interested in the relationship between intellectual philosophy and the psyche of the philosopher, once de-

---

20. Georges Lemaître, *From Cubism to Surrealism,* p. 183.

fined absurd comedy as the spectacle of someone who sees what he has been trained to think he sees rather than what is really before his eyes.[21] A pompous fool of a general in *The Wedding on the Eiffel Tower* reasons that "there can be no lion on-the Eiffel Tower" and that, therefore, the one he sees is a mirage —until it eats him. The surrealists amused themselves hugely with the reflection that whereas everyone else (especially their parents' generation) loved the Eiffel Tower in the delusion that it represented rationality, only they were clear-sighted enough to see that it represented many aspects of nonrationality—and still to love it. Whereas everyone else insisted on seeing logical order in the universe, they exulted in perceiving the opposite and laughed at those who clung to blindness.

This gleeful repudiation of rationality, and of a society predicated on rationality within a technological context, was the basis of Dada and surrealism. On this basis, first Dada and then surrealism built consistent ideational structures.

21. It is a very special inversion of common sense. It consists in seeking to mold things on an idea of one's own, instead of molding one's ideas on things— in seeing before us what we are thinking of, instead of thinking of what we see . . . reality . . . has to bow to imagination—Henri Bergson, *Comedy*, p. 179.

CHAPTER TWO

Dada and Surrealism

Dada and surrealism were born out of the artists' awareness of a society gone haywire and clinging to rational explanations of increasingly irrational twentieth-century experiences, chief among which was World War One. They were closely linked attempts to be fully conscious of their own participation in the rush toward chaos. And their particular genius lay not only in their vision but also in their determination to enjoy the whole experience.

There was a theatricality in surrealist life and art. One critic has observed that in retrospect they have "begun to look like a twenty-year mock-heroic morality play whose structure and detail convey the turbulence we increasingly churn up around us."[1] Even the historians who never mention this theatricality seem to feel it. The surrealists' most hostile contemporaries could not resist watching the show; and neither can posterity. Dada and surrealism thought of themselves naturally in theatrical metaphors, as when a Dada manifesto proclaimed: "We . . . are preparing the great spectacle of disaster, arson, decomposition."[2] Later we will see specific connections between surrealism and the theater (and film). For now, let us establish the image of a group

1. Roger Shattuck, "Surrealism Reappraised," in Nadeau, *History of Surrealism*, p. 28, n. 3.
2. "Nous . . . préparons le grand spectacle de désastre, d'incendie, la décomposition." Tristan Tzara, "Le manifeste dada," 1918, in *Lampisteries précédées de sept manifestes Dada*, p. 19.

of performers representing their audience through a primitive sacred spectacle.

Dada "exploded like a well-timed bomb"[3] in Zurich in 1917, and two years later Tristan Tzara brought it to Paris where new converts were already waiting impatiently. Dada was a philosophy which, in life and art, tried to use existing intellectual and material conditions in the same way as contemporaneous practitioners of modern dance were learning to use the floor; to push from, to refer to while in flight away from. In fact, Dada found its entire raison d'être in this motion *away*. Dada denied meaning to any other direction—denied the possibility of rational meaningfulness in the abstract—and expended its collective energy in dissociation and negation, in mocking with obscene gestures society and intellect and art, all illusions of an era too pigheaded to confront its chaos. Like dancers, Dadaists integrated into the motion of their lives and art the accelerating whirl of dis-equilibrium which they sensed gathering around them.

Dada's ideal was nothingness; almost the only act it respected was suicide; and one reason for the collapse of the organization was that organizational continuity was counter to the spirit of their principles. Another reason was that absolutely consistent negation turned out to be an extremely difficult attitude to sustain the members' work and lives.

By 1921, Dada members who felt the need for some positive principles for action and creation had begun to adapt Dada to their need. Some historians date the surrealists' final break with Dada from a 1923 performance of Tristan Tzara's *The Gas Heart* (*Le Coeur à Gaz*), which erupted into a brawl between Dada faithful, surrealist dissenters, and the police; others feel that the crucial occasion was the 1921 mock trial of Maurice Barrès, an established writer of reactionary tendencies whom Dada was try-

3. Calvin Tomkins, *The Bride and the Bachelors: Five Masters of the Avant-Garde*, p. 44.

ing, in the person of a tailor's dummy, for a long list of moral and literary crimes. In any case, the new group developed independently while still carrying on many of Dada's techniques and assumptions. They imposed a "theoretical and methodical infrastructure" on the Dada gesture and "codified the Dada revolt into a strict intellectual discipline."[4] By 1924 the group was sufficiently established to warrant an official name of its own. André Breton, the group's leader, picked up Guillaume Apollinaire's term "surrealism" and stretched it to fit an entire new aesthetic and philosophical movement.

Apollinaire, who was dead by then, had coined the word in 1917 in program notes to the Diaghilev-Picasso-Satie-Massine ballet *Parade* to signify an aesthetic "point of departure for a series of manifestations of New Spirit that . . . promises to transform arts and manners into universal joy." (He had continued mischievously that "common sense" demands that arts and manners be "at least on a level with scientific and industrial progress.")[5] Apollinaire's "New Spirit" of joy was thus integral to the Surrealist movement from its birth. The surrealists believed in joy. Although they were angry at society, they adopted energetic optimism in place of Dada sullenness. Antonin Artaud suggested the ebullience of the movement when he wrote that "Surrealism rose up in cocktails/an Eiffel Tower of alcohol."[6] Indeed,

---

4. Hans Richter, *Dada: Art and Anti-Art*, p. 195.

5. Apollinaire articulated the concept of the "New Spirit" most fully at a conference on the subject, "The New Spirit and the Poets," held in 1917 in the Vieux-Colombier Theater in Paris. In the Prologue to his play *The Breasts of Tiresias*, performed the same year, he speaks of "joyfulness voluptuousness virtue," expressions of the New Spirit. Apollinaire preached this concept as a reaction against wartime gloom: "to light again the stars" which "cannon" had extinguished.

After Apollinaire further developed the term "surrealism" in the Preface to the same play, Yvan Goll seems to have been the first to adopt this usage, writing in an essay on Mallarmé in 1918 that "The work of art must make reality more real (surréaliser la realité)"—in *Trois bons esprits de France*, (Berlin: Editions Erich Reiss, n.d.)

6.   Le Surréalisme monté dans les cocktails,
                    une tour Eiffel d'alcool;

Antonin Artaud, *Deux Nations sur les confins de la Mongolie* . . . (scenario) in *Oeuvres Complètes*, III, p. 17.

besides the existence of the "theoretical and methodical infrastructure," this lift in emotional atmosphere is the only essential difference between Dada and surrealism.

The surrealists' characteristic mode was "le merveilleux"—the marvelous—which signified to them a gleeful freedom of the imagination, a general liberation and purification within an acceptance of material reality, and a capacity for childlike wonder and fresh response. The very word "marvelous" is a motif which appears again and again in all surrealist thinking. Luis Buñuel applied it to film; Eugene Ionesco was to use it later for theater. René Magritte, the painter, said that "the principal value of Surrealism seems to me to be that it has reintroduced the marvelous into everyday possibilities. It has taught that if reality seemed . . . flat, it is because man did not know how to see, his glance was limited by an education deliberately intended to blind him and by an aesthetic censor inherited from past ages."[7] Magritte's happy feeling for the "mystery of the familiar world in which we live"[8] is comparable to Breton's exultant litany: "The marvelous is always beautiful, anything marvelous at all is beautiful, nothing but the marvelous is beautiful."[9] Apollinaire's personal "devise" had been simply "I marvel!" The excitement of the marvelous in surrealism was only heightened by the constant presence of its own dark side: the violent anger which was Dada's legacy.

In other words, surrealism was largely composed of formerly Dada ideas and members. As a staunch Dadaist was to write, some forty years later and still resentful, "Surrealism devoured and digested Dada":[10] a circumstance which makes it extremely difficult for us to distinguish consistently between former Dadaists

7. J. H. Matthews, *An Introduction to Surrealism*, p. 144.
8. *Fantasmagie*, Nos. 3–4 (1959), p. 59, quoted in Matthews, ibid., p. 144.
9. "Le merveilleux est toujours beau, n'importe quel merveilleux est beau, il n'y a même que le merveilleux qui soit beau." André Breton, *First Surrealist Manifesto*, in *Les Manifestes du Surréalisme* (Paris, 1955), p. 16.
10. Richter, *Dada*, p. 194.

and their surrealist works. But these formerly Dada ideas and members were so altered by the basic shift from negative to positive attitudes that Dada may actually be said to have been transformed into something entirely new. In musical terms we might say, loosely, that the surrealists transposed Dada from minor into major, and thereby made the tune quite different.

The transformation from negative to positive underlies all aspects of surrealism. Both Dada and the Surrealist movement violently repudiated a society predicated upon rationality, and both attempted to derive from this attitude a larger world view. But whereas Dada glimpsed dimly a world essence beyond rationality, the surrealists postulated such an essence more fully and called this semi-mystical concept surreality.

Both Dada and surrealism, especially the latter, envisaged a dichotomy of extremes between this surreality and objective reality. Surreality is a kind of internal or universal reality, whereas objective reality is composed of phenomena which are visible to all and are chaotic and trivial. Both extremes of reality are equally nonrational. They were conceived as separated from each other by the non-real barrier of reason and of rationally ordered social existence. Thus rationality and order were related only negatively to universal truths.

Ironically, despite their scorn for conventional intellectual activity, Dada and the Surrealist movement shared philosophy's traditional ambition to comprehend in some sense the structure of the universe. Dada, being a static program, incorporated no real longing to find and experience the truth, however. Dada remained negative: pure repudiation. But surrealism, on the other hand, was dynamic, rooted in a spirit of regeneration rather than flat disillusionment, and consciously fighting to attain in some way the universal truths beyond philosophy.

If rationality and conventional social behavior actually stood between a man and his understanding of the truth, then obviously the Western traditionally intellectual means of attaining truth were useless or worse. Dada and surrealism had deliberately rejected even for their own use the intellectual tools of society; reason, they claimed, is a habit and a sham. But, surrealism postulated more or less consciously, if the barrier of rationality were dissolved or blasted away or at least circumvented, there would follow a sudden unprecedented confrontation of the two extremes of reality. For an instant, they would unite; and a glimpse of the ultimate reality, or essence, or surreality, would result. Thus nonrational knowledge would be achieved nonrationally, and an intense experience, both personal and universal, would emerge from chaotic nothingness.

The drive basic to surrealism is toward such a reconciliation of opposites. This drive is a constant and applies to all the various dichotomies of the surrealist world view: the idea and the concrete, the eternal and the immediate, the universe and the individual. In each case the two extremes must be reconciled in order for either one to fulfill, however briefly, its own nature. This formulation reminds us of Hegel's thesis-antithesis-synthesis; but there is no record that the surrealists themselves noticed the similarity.

Reconciliation refers both to a formulated perception of the universe and to an intense experience of that perception. As always in surrealist thinking, formulation is worthless except through experience. So all surrealist effort was bent on inducing the experience by various techniques. Of course, an experience of such intensity, involving so precarious a reconciliation of opposites, was by its nature impossible to prolong more than an instant in time. Thus reconciliation was an intensification in time as well as in spirit, a way to assimilate Bergsonian duration in time. The tension inherent in the willed unification of opposites which are straining apart lent a kind of quivering energy to all the movement's activities.

The paradigmatic surrealist experience of reconciliation was provided by art. It is true that Dada had dismissed art along with all the rest of society's respected institutions; "Art," wrote Jacques Vaché, presumably with a lordly wave of his hand, "is imbecility."[11] Certainly Dada and surrealism both were considered by their members to be primarily philosophies and ways of life rather than schools of art. Nevertheless the great majority of these adherents were practicing artists or poets, who are in fact now remembered best and with most affection for their art works. For the principles with which members of Dada and the Surrealist movement began seemed inevitably to draw artists as members and to lead members to practice art. Apollinaire used the word "surrealism" in the Prologue to his play *The Breasts of Tiresias* to mean, precisely, "a tendency in art."[12]

The solution of this paradox of dismissal of and commitment to art lies in a tacit redefinition of art begun by Dada. Art was no longer the creation of something. For Dada, art was a gesture, usually expressing rejection of society (including the spectator). Art was not the antithesis of life; art was part of living.

The Surrealist movement carried the redefinition further. For the surrealist artist, art is an experience of creation which includes, in the same instant: first, the artist's perception of sur-reality, through the taking-form of some art work; and second, the reconciliation of the artist with his audience through the art work, so that their perception of surreality is mutual and simultaneous. Artistic creation is thus a concentrated personal experience of surreality for artist and spectator, and surrealist art works constitute the momentary triumph of positive assertion over a conviction of nothingness. They are containers of the experience,

---

11. "L'art est une sottise." Jacques Vaché, *Lettres de la Guerre*, p. 20.
12. Pour caractériser mon drame je me suis servi d'un néologisme . . . et j'ai forgé l'adjectif surréaliste qui . . . définit assez bien une tendence de l'art. . . .
"Préface" to *Les Mamelles de Tirésias* in *Oeuvres Complètes*, p. 865.

proofs of such an experience in the past, and talismans to such an experience in the future.

One source of the Surrealist movement's particular affinity with the theater lies in the fact that the theater is after all the one art form which absolutely demands that creation be in the form of an immediate experience by an artist together with the immediate presence and participation of the spectator—who is even, in a sense, sharing the artist's experience. It is an art whose "image," in painter Marcel Duchamp's definition of all surrealist art, is not a "thing" but "an act" and one "which must be completed by the spectator."[13] We might also say that the surrealist notion of art and life involved literally "acting out," with concentration and energy, a vision of the world which they shared with the rest of society, their audience. In fact, the theatricality of the Surrealist movement was so assimilated into the members' practice of the arts that it did not demand expression necessarily through formal plays.

We should also note here another connection which will continue to appear in later chapters. Both as a form of drama and as a technological art form as new as surrealism itself, cinema—all cinema—is to some extent inherently surrealist. André Breton once commented that it was in the movie theater that "is celebrated the only absolutely modern mystery."[14] Obviously he was using "mystère" in the Catholic sense of sacred spectacle, with the surrealists the first and purest celebrants.

Because it is through art, both dramatic and non-dramatic, that surrealist experiences were accessible to surrealists, and because it is through art that such experiences can be observed after the fact by outsiders like us, we will study surrealism

13. Katherine S. Dreier and Matta Echaurreu, *Duchamp's Glass: An Analytical Reflection.*
14. "C'est là [au cinéma] que se célèbre le seul mystère absolument moderne." Breton, quoted in Aldo Kyrou, *Le Surréalisme au Cinéma,* p. 22.

through the surrealist experience. We will approach this experience by looking at the surrealist artist first, then at his art works, and then at his relationship with his audience.

Max Ernst, *Loplop Introduces Members of the Surrealist Group* (1930). Collage of photographs and pencil. The top row shows, left to right: Tanguy (whistling or making faces, his hair apparently blowing in the wind), Aragon, Giacometti, Crevel. Hand points down to Ernst and, next to him, Dali. Tzara stands behind Dali's elbow. Buñuel is below, walking with his hands in his sweater pockets. Nearby Eluard wears a hat and smokes. At the bottom are Man Ray just above the big hand and Breton apparently drowning in the center. Collection, the Museum of Modern Art, New York.

One of a series of tableaux vivants in a "story without words" meant to express the spirit of surrealist hi-jinks. Composed and acted by Artaud and Vitrac and a Mlle. Lusson. Photographs appear in a manifesto entitled *Le Théâtre Alfred-Jarry et L'Hostilité Publique* (1930). Courtesy of Annabelle Henkin.

CHAPTER THREE

The Surrealist Artist

At the heart of surrealist philosophy was the individual surrealist life experience, as crystallized in artistic creation. Identifying the artist by his eccentric life style as well as by his work was increasingly conventional throughout the nineteenth century: part of the romantic tradition. But the surrealists went further; they were artists, as we have seen, primarily because art was for them a means of living the surrealist life with intense awareness. In fact, the surrealist artist felt (like his contemporary Isadora Duncan and near-contemporary Oscar Wilde) that one's self is his primary artistic creation and must be fully achieved. The preoccupation with life style, something of a commonplace today, was fresh with them. This extension of the surrealist redefinition of art made it possible for many surrealists to be esteemed by their fellows as proven artists without having produced anything at all but their own surrealist personalities. Later in this chapter we will investigate surrealists, especially Antonin Artaud, one of the most famous, and an artist by any definition. For we must get an idea of how the surrealist artist lived and worked in order to understand his art.

Since to the surrealist artist surrealism was above all a philosophy of life, his proudest boast was that he lived it out purely. The surrealists cultivated personality as the Byronesque romantics had done. They were bold eccentrics, though they varied in style from Alfred Jarry's formal vulgarities to Apollinaire's rather precious lyricism. Their deliberate magnification of the personality, and their emphasis on the individual's bursting through convention did differ in one way from the romantics' approach, however: its moral tone was higher or at least more self-conscious. True, the surrealists enjoyed their own flamboyance, and they enjoyed affronting the bourgeoisie. They enjoyed the release from the constraint of rational behavior. But, also, they believed that their silliness contained some nobility and served as a rebuke to logic.

This is how composer Erik Satie described his life style:

An artist must regulate his life. Here is my precise daily schedule. I rise at 7:18; am inspired from 10:30 to 11:47. . . . A healthy horseback ride on my property from 1:19 to 2:35. . . .

Dinner is served at 7:16 and finished at 7:20. Afterward from 8:09 to 9:59 symphonic readings out loud.

I go to bed regularly at 10:37. Once a week I wake up with a start at 3:15 A.M. (Tuesdays).

I eat only white foods: eggs, sugar, shredded bones, the fat of dead animals, rice. . . .

I breathe carefully (a little at a time) and dance very rarely. When walking I hold my sides and look steadily behind me. . . .

I sleep with only one eye closed; I sleep very hard. My bed is round with a hole in it for my head to go through. Every hour a servant takes my temperature and gives me another.

For a long time I have subscribed to a fashion magazine. I wear a white cap, white socks, and a white vest.

My doctor has always told me to smoke. He even explains himself: "Smoke, my friend. Otherwise someone else will smoke in your place."[1]

1. Roger Shattuck, *The Banquet Years*, pp. 179–80.

Obviously this not an objective account. But an objective biography of almost any surrealist would include such tidbits as Eluard's impulsive departure for Tahiti; Breton's affectation of a monocle on some days and big green spectacles on others; Dadaist boxer Arthur Cravan's deliberate undressing onstage before a group of startled ladies and his final disappearance in a small boat off the coast of South America; Breton's and Vaché's army leaves spent together stumbling from one movie theater directly into another; the popular surrealist practice of riding an unattractive suburban train route all day to nowhere and back again.

One reason the surrealists behaved eccentrically and obscenely in public was in the hope that their aesthetic-philosophical stance would improve society, first spiritually and then inevitably in more tangible ways. Angry at society, they were determined to make their lives instruments for flaunting society. Herbert Read connects the surrealist impulse to social revolution with the Marxian proposition that "the object of philosophy is not to interpret the world but to transform it," and with the capacity of the Marxian dialectic "to pass from the static to the dynamic."[2] Certainly the surrealists advocated a collapse of social distinctions along with all other bourgeois institutions, including established art and artists; typically they called Goethe a clown[3] and claimed that if you read André Gide's works aloud for ten minutes "your mouth will smell bad."[4] The *Funeral March* composed by Honegger for Cocteau's *The Wedding on the Eiffel Tower* was the only part of the play praised by some critics, who thus fell into a deliberate trap; none of them recognized a parody of the "Waltz" from *Faust*. But from a dialectic within which politics and art merge with the other elements of an organic social system, surrealism envisioned a general liberation and purification.

2. Herbert Read, *Art and Society*, pp. 120–21. Read prefers the term "superrealism" to refer to the same movement.
3. Nadeau, *History of Surrealism*, p. 147.
4. Francis Picabia, quoted in Nadeau, ibid., p. 63.

Politics too could be a natural expression of the surrealist life style. But we should mention here that even to the extent that surrealists were politically oriented, they were anarchists rather than practical reformers. (Anarchism has of course a long tradition in France.) Indeed they considered themselves the more subversive in that they were not content to attack the unjust and irrational, but rather that they attacked justice and rationality. While Dada was purely nihilistic, however, surrealism was more activist. In 1927, the movement even went so far as to pronounce itself officially "in the service of the Revolution." But its official association with the Communist party was quarrelsome, confused, and brief. Eventually, as its charter members themselves grew older and developed more prosperous stakes, the movement's program was to grow somewhat more positive toward society. During the World War Two period, moreover, many of the leading surrealists were forced to flee France, which meant perhaps that they simply lost all possibilities for continuing social activism in a familiar context. In any case, from the beginning, surrealism's identity as a group was rooted in its role as embattled minority in bourgeois society, so that adverse reaction served as a catalyst for reaffirmation of the group; and this lasted even after the bourgeoisie had largely accepted the surrealist vision.

The quality of surrealists' lives managed to combine with this anger their feeling for the marvelous always present in their philosophy. Even their pranks and obscenities had an aura of youthful high spirits. They had fun at parties posing for group photos in silly costumes. The clown was a favored motif for several of them, as it was in the 1930s for Picasso, always the first to sketch new lines of interest. They loved practical jokes and puns. Duchamp carried on ruthlessly punning correspondences with friends, and once he paid a large dentist bill with a check drawn on "The Teeth's Loan and Trust Company, Consolidated."

The surrealists believed in love. A manifesto included in the program of the opening of the film *Age of Gold* (*L'Age d'Or*) proclaimed that:

. . . The day will come when we realize that . . . the very corner-stone of that violent liberation which reaches out for a cleaner life in the heart of the technological age that corrupts our cities is,

LOVE. . . .[5]

The obscenities which delighted the surrealists, and with which they insisted on shocking people, also had an element of genuine celebration of love, especially physical love, which seemed to them the perfect metaphor for union and the momentary climactic blissful union of opposites. Indeed for some surrealists, woman took on an almost mystical sexual power "to mediate between man and the marvelous."[6] Éluard and others played at chivalric anatomizations in lyric praise of their sweethearts' beauties. In January of 1928 the movement held a formal conference devoted to sex, in particular to heterosexual love as preferable to homosexual. Strong friendship between men was one of their prime values, however, and indeed the core of the movement was the personal affection and respect between them. An early sympathetic critic describing the surrealists to a French public still unfamiliar with them found it important to mention along with their art style "the friendship" which they "cultivate and boast of."[7]

This same critic compared surrealism—for better and worse— to "the strange prolongation of a crisis of adolescence." Certainly we should point out that all the members of the Surrealist movement (except the composer Satie, who was, as we shall see,

5. From the manifesto included in the program of Luis Buñuel's film *L'Age d'Or* and signed by Aragon, Breton, Crevel, Dali, Éluard, Péret, Tzara, and others. In Luis Buñuel, *L'Age d'Or* and *Un Chien Andalou*, translated by Marianne Alexandre (New York: Simon and Schuster, 1968), p. 7.

6. Matthews, *Introduction*, p. 163.

7. Jean Cassou, "Propos sur le surréalisme," *La Nouvelle Revue Française*, January 1, 1925, p. 34.

an exception in several ways) were quite young men who were, moreover, extremely conscious of the youth of the century and the age. Their peers Alain-Fournier (*Le Grand Meaulnes* or *The Lost Domain* or *The Wanderer*) and Radiguet (*Le Diable au Corps* or *Devil in the Flesh*) wrote romantic tales of the pain of adolescent love in classically melancholy provincial French settings; coincidentally, both these authors wrote one lovely novel and died young. This fictional genre, which is traditional in French literature, is much gentler than the surrealist atmosphere, but seems related in feeling nonetheless. Radiguet also wrote a surrealist comedy called *The Pelicans*.

Men who had grandly independent and antisocial personalities were the surrealists' heroes. The Marquis de Sade was a special favorite; it was Apollinaire who resurrected his writings from the Paris library archives and edited them, and the Luis Buñuel film *Age of Gold*, on which Salvador Dali also worked for a time, contains a Sade-like character dressed like Jesus. Alfred Jarry was another favorite; so was Rimbaud; and so was Isidore Ducasse, who called himself the Comte de Lautréamont. So was Jacques Vaché, Breton's army friend, who produced almost nothing but a series of letters which were later published by his friends, but who dressed fastidiously, swore grossly, despised everything, and killed himself at twenty-two, before the Surrealist movement took shape.

Thus, unlike most philosophic stances, surrealism could be sustained and actually lived by for long periods. Perhaps this was possible because a totally surrealist life includes within itself all minor distractions such as concrete impressions, the search for physical comforts, eccentricities of dress, lapses of dignity and good temper, lapses of productive power, personal hostilities, small daily pleasures of all sorts, loves and friendships and their endings—everything, in short, but conventionality (unless in a spirit of mockery) and moderation.

The art works which the surrealist artist produced were touch-
stones of his personal experiences of surreality. Unconsciously
echoing—or parodying—Longinus' dictum that "sublimity in
art is the echo of a noble mind,"[8] the surrealists believed that
only a fully surrealist personality can create a fully surrealist art
work.

Naturally, therefore, the surrealists respected only those artists
of the past as seemed to them to have achieved surreality in life
style as well as in work; and only a shifting list of these managed
to escape the surrealists' scorn at last. The most permanent, besides those poets mentioned above, were Hieronymus Bosch and
William Blake, who both were personally antisocial and also
somewhat hallucinatory in style. All others, especially of the
generation of the surrealists' parents, were automatically suspect.
Even Apollinaire was accused, as early as 1919, of conservatism:
"We no longer know who Apollinaire is—BECAUSE—we suspect him of . . . patching up romanticism with telephone wire,
. . . not knowing that the dynamos, the STARS, are still disconnected."[9]

So deeply interrelated were creator and creation that the distinction between them blurred for the surrealists. Sometimes the
artist and art work actually merged. For example, Alfred Jarry,
the proto-surrealist who died in 1907, maintained the high tragi-
comic surrealist life style right up to his deathbed request, to a
circle of grieving friends, for—a toothpick. Jarry produced a
number of plays which are surrealist in style, especially the *King
Ubu (Ubu Roi)* series. And the culmination of his surrealist self
was that he actually visibly became his hero Ubu, developing the
potbelly, the stentorian voice, the predilection for duels and grand
pronouncements for which Ubu was famous. Similarly, though on

8. Longinus, *'Longinus': On Sublimity*, p. 9.
9. Jacques Vaché (always an extremist), quoted in Nadeau, *History of Surrealism*, p. 59.

a much more superficial level, we see that Marcel Duchamp took on a punning pseudonym—an artist named Rrose Sélavy (read it aloud)—and maintained her existence, elaborately, for years. Man Ray's photograph of the lady shows her wearing lipstick, a turban, and a grimly genteel expression; but the nose is unmistakably Duchamp's. (We might recall at this point, too, that the Eiffel Tower has immortalized the name of its creator, who planned and directed the entire undertaking and who has disappeared for posterity except through his Tower.)

Antonin Artaud may be called the ultimate surrealist. He surpassed Jarry, both in the magnificence of his surrealist stance and in his effort to articulate surrealist formulae (which had, after all, hardly existed in any coherent form in Jarry's day). He was capable of sustained existence and productivity at a unique pitch of absolute surreality. The posthumous expansion of his personality into a cult myth can only be evidence of the force of the surrealist ethos today. The particularly surrealist strength of his work is inseparable from the circumstance that he lived a perfectly surrealist life. In fact he followed surrealist principles in their pure form right out of the organizational framework of the Surrealist movement, carrying the surrealist attitude of rebellion to the extreme of rebelling against the movement, with resultant permanent hard feelings on both sides. He wrote *In the Dark of the Night or The Surrealist Bluff*, among other polemical pamphlets and articles, denouncing the movement's remaining members.

It is an indication of how fully Artaud integrated the surrealist life style within his personal identity that discussion of any of his works seems inevitably to take a different form from discussion of other artists' works, even including other surrealist plays. In order to deal with the uniquely personal quality of Artaud's works, it seems to become necessary to move into another, more personal and more spiritual dimension—which is precisely what the philosophy of surrealism demanded: that every act of creation be absolutely personal; that creator and creation be one; and, further, that the conventional artificial distinction between art and life in the abstract be dissolved. Similarly, Proust, whose life was somewhat in the surrealist mode, used his life and personality as the basis of his art so that his biography and his novel are almost inseparable.

We can see Artaud as paradigmatic surrealist and surrealist artist by looking at him in relation to an example of his work: the short scenario *Jet of Blood:* a disconnected series of violently emotional actions involving a Young Man and other characters (Young Girl, Nurse, Knight, Whore), all in a lurid nightmare fantasy world. This play is inextricably bound up with its author's surrealist being in several ways, all of which merge with and feed each other.

First of all, Artaud was not a rational man. Probably the one fact most often cited about him in any connection is that he was mad. Jerzy Grotowski, founder of the Polish Laboratory Theater, which is both avant-garde and in some ways surrealist, approaches his definition of Artaud's contribution to the theatre with this statement: "Artaud teaches us a great lesson. . . . This lesson is his madness."[10] Surrealism as a whole, rejecting rationality for the richer energies which lay beyond, was fascinated by madness. It has been suggested that the movement collectively was possessed, according to a primitive concept of holy madness in which one man expresses the madness of his entire community and thereby purges it; a Freudian analogy would be a therapeutic kind of acting-out for the sake of ultimate sanity. Artaud, embodying such madness throughout a lifetime and creating only out of this madness, embodies a surrealist idea; by virtue of this, his creations, which share his identity, have special surrealist validity.

10. Jerzy Grotowski, *Towards a Poor Theatre,* p. 123.

More specifically this madness presumably shaped his work. Bettina Knapp speculates that Artaud's mental condition made concentrated logical thinking impossible, and Artaud himself wrote: "I suffer from a frightful disease of the mind. My thought abandons me at all stages."[11] (The hero of his scenario *18 Seconds* has the same problem.)

Not only did Artaud's madness underlie his work by definition, simply because the creator was mad; his work is even hallucinatory in style, plot, and form. Again *Jet of Blood* provides an example. Characters miss contact in hallucinatory fashion. The pace and selection of images possible to film intensify the highly colored nightmare atmosphere; flying limbs and colonnades, slowly moving insects, transformations of hair into flame. The atmosphere is violent, as in the central image of a spurt of blood and in the desperation of all the emotions expressed. The atmosphere is also erotic. Breasts and genitals are a constant motif and seem to wield power over the characters.

Rebelliousness was part of the surrealist attitude, and Artaud was rebellious by nature; he even rebelled against surrealism. When producing Strindberg's *A Dream Play*, Artaud said "Strindberg revolted . . . as I have. We are producing this play as vomit against society."[12] Rebelliousness is inherent in the action of *Jet of Blood*, where the harsh swift impact of the cinematic series of images makes the rebelliousness seem particularly savage. Specifically, Artaud mocks bourgeois institutions: maternal tenderness, in the person of the Nurse's grotesque breasts; the panoply of history, culture, honor, in the person of the infantile Knight; the Church in the person of the Priest. Really there is only one major surrealist characteristic which is not typical of Artaud: a sense of the marvelous. And even though his work—and personality—lack the gay freshness, the friskiness

11. Bettina Knapp, *Antonin Artaud*, p. 11.
12. Ibid., p. 410, n. 26.

and verve, of the marvelous which we see in *The Wedding on the Eiffel Tower* and most other surrealist works, they do nevertheless have its sense of multicolored mystery.

It is particularly useful for us to choose a dramatist, like Artaud, to discuss as a typical surrealist artist since, to play with words (and the surrealists loved to play with words), in art as in life surrealists were constantly engaged in dramatizing themselves. They were constantly performing, reading writings aloud, exhibiting paintings and sculpture as part of performances, bending efforts in painting and sculpture deliberately toward scenery and costumes for performances.

And the surrealist artist's own personality, dramatized, generally dominated his own work. This is perhaps the corollary of the work's swallowing the personality, as with Jarry's *Ubu*. René Magritte peopled some of his paintings with stocky bourgeois in black business suits and bowler hats—replicas of himself. Sometimes whimsical, sometimes threatening (especially when they appear in numbers), they eventually took on the quality of a symbol of ambiguous reference.[13] The Douanier Henri Rousseau, not a surrealist but an early influence upon them and a friend of Apollinaire's, appears in many of his own paintings, tucked into corners as if to say in person a characteristically cheerful hello.[14] Luis Buñuel and Salvador Dali both appear in their film *Un Chien Andalou* (*An Andalusian Dog*).

The implication of Artaud's original career, which was not as dramatist but as actor, is that he had deliberately committed himself to a profession in which he would act creation out, literally embody the creative act, and participate in person at the precise

13. For example: *L'assassin menacé* (1926–27) at the Museum of Modern Art in New York, and *Les rêveries du promeneur solitaire* (1926–27) in the collection of E. L. T. Mesens in Brussels.
14. Roger Shattuck describes these "miniatures in broad-brimmed hats, . . . tiny black shapes, . . . little men with canes" as Rousseau's "emblematic presence in the scenes he paints." Shattuck, *Banquet Years*, p. 97.

moment at which the audience receives the creation. Painters, sculptors, poets do not have such a perfect surrealist experience. The only professional actor among the active surrealists—almost the only actor even associated with the movement (Roger Blin was the other)—Artaud was thus close to the perfect surrealist state and so, therefore, were his plays and performances. Henri Béhar attempts to explain the conspicuous absence of actors in the Surrealist movement by reference to André Breton's horror of duplicity and role-playing of all kinds.[15]

Another aspect of this self-dramatization lies in the fact that although the surrealists claimed to have rejected all literary conventions, including plot and characters, most of their plays do have definite protagonists representative of the author. The hero's presence in plays and films has a function integrally connected with the surrealist conceptions of art. The hero's very existence onstage allows the dramatist whom he represents to live onstage; to *be* his own creation, by proxy, despite the alien presence of the actor. Thus the playwright can carry to its ultimate the surrealist tendency to self-dramatization. Sometimes even the author is a character, as in *The Mysteries of Love* by Roger Vitrac, during which he appears several times: once he is covered with blood after his offstage suicide, and laughing uncontrollably; later he discusses the play with the characters. In Tristan Tzara's play *The First Heavenly Adventure of Mr. Aspirin*, the author himself acted a character named Tristan Tzara.

The hero in Dada surrealist plays and films (the surrealists wrote almost no novels) strongly resembles traditional romantic heroes of the school of Victor Hugo's play *Hernani*. Patrice in *The Mysteries of Love*, The Poet in *Handkerchief Cloud* by Tzara, Maxime in *La Place de L'Étoile* by Desnos—all are young, mysterious, suffering, doomed, in love, and usually beloved. All reveal

---

15. Henri Béhar, "La Question du Théâtre Surréaliste, ou le Théâtre en Question," *Europe*, p. 164.

poetic soulfulness, melancholy, loneliness, pride, bitterness, flamboyance, mystical moral stature, and attractiveness to women. Remember that the surrealists were all young men. Of course these romantic traits recall the public pose which was de rigueur for them. Rimbaud and the other *poètes maudits*, whose spiritual heirs the surrealists considered themselves to be, fit this romantic mold perfectly. Jarry and Vaché, the surrealists' particular idols, did too, with only the addition of an aggressive playfulness of manner.

In Artaud's *Jet of Blood*, the protagonist is called simply the Young Man, and he goes even beyond the stereotype to share such specific aspects of Artaud's own personality as horror of sex (as in his reaction to the Nurse's revealing her genitals), yearning toward mystical knowledge (as in his conversation with the Priest), and hostility toward parental figures (as in his treatment of the Nurse and the Knight, who are the Young Girl's parents).[16]

As a dramatist, Artaud grappled with a problem in surrealist aesthetics. There is a special insight to be gained by discussing the surrealist creator in the sphere of drama. A poem, painting, or sculpture is clearly the work of a single artist: a single, perhaps instantaneous, creative experience. But a dramatist must reckon with a whole community of co-workers in other media; actors, director, designer, and so on. And all these work at different moments. (Music distinguishes similarly between composer and performer.) We cannot fail to see how consistently surrealist artists connected in any way with the theater groped, consciously or unconsciously, toward a unification of these discrete experiences into a single creator: the "universal athlete" who can do all the composing and performing, as visualized by Jean Cocteau.[17]

16. Bettina Knapp calls the play "a revelation . . . of the difficulties he had in making his adjustments as a boy becoming a man," but this seems an oversimplification at any level. Knapp, *Artaud*, p. 32.
17. ". . . un athlète complet," Jean Cocteau, "Introduction" to *Les Mariés de la Tour Eiffel* in *Théâtre* (Paris: Sans Pareil), p. 48.

Artaud offers only one of many examples of this compulsion to absorb entire creative experience into a single artist, despite the pull of the art form out toward multiplicity. Often, for example, the entire company of a surrealist theater effort were good friends and worked together as one; their personal intimacy welded them into a single "universal athlete." This was the practical compromise which Cocteau himself suggested. Another way was for a single artist to function in as many aspects of the production as possible. Apollinaire not only wrote *The Breasts of Tiresias* but also gathered the creation into his own personal identity by directing it and by appearing in it as a character named The Director (by proxy only, since an actor played the part) to speak the Prologue which described his own experiences in the trenches. The spoken lines of Tristan Tzara's play *The Gas Heart,* which he wrote and in which he acted, include stage directions, usually delivered by the same speaker, such as "A little more life down there onstage." In order to reduce the number of participants by eliminating live creative actors, several surrealist dramatists, such as Pierre Albert-Birot,[18] experimented with marionettes. Even Jarry had originally written *King Ubu* for marionettes. We ought to remember, though, that in all this the surrealists were adopting a tendency already abroad in the West: the omnipotent director, also exemplified by Reinhardt, Wagner, Granville Barker, and Gordon Craig (who was especially interested in the possibilities of marionette theater).

Artaud accomplished this unification of the creative act in several ways. First, by making of his career overall an almost total theater experience, he worked out in his own person the conflict which is inevitable, according to surrealist theory, between

---

18. Pierre Albert-Birot envisioned a "théâtre nunique" which he described in 1916 in *SIC,* a magazine which he edited and in which he printed a lot of early surrealist work. Apollinaire acknowledged Albert-Birot's influence on his own thinking about theater.

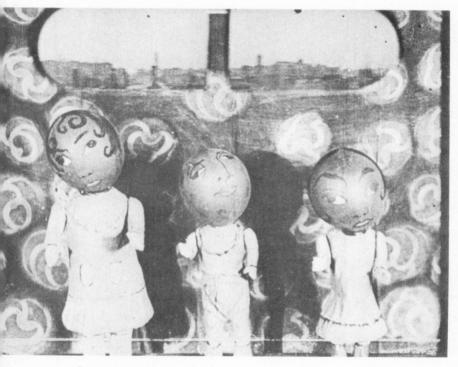

From René Clair's film *Entr'acte (Intermission)*. These puppets' heads are balloons, and later the three will simultaneously deflate, each grimacing, shriveling, and finally sagging onto the right shoulder. Permission Cinémathèque Française, Paris.

Spaces, shadows, dimensions suggest a dream. Note the train far in the background. Giorgio de Chirico, *The Enigma of a Day* (1914). Oil. James Thrall Soby Collection at the Museum of Modern Art, New York. Courtesy of Mr. Soby.

creative participants in a single theater event. By the time he wrote *Jet of Blood,* Artaud had already unified in his own personal career a total artistic experience. He had been an actor for years. He had directed and designed, especially for a theater which he himself organized, the Théâtre Alfred-Jarry. And he wrote plays, scenarios, aesthetic speculations about the theater. Often he combined functions simultaneously, as when he played Count Cenci in his own production of his own play *The Cenci—* which was, by the way, the only production of the Theater of Cruelty.

Artaud found another solution, perhaps the solution of the future, to this conflict between creators when he turned to film. Here the director was indeed, in several ways, sole creator. Many of Artaud's works were specifically written as film scenarios. Artaud felt throughout most of his career what Apollinaire had glimpsed long before: that a new cinematographic sensibility was "one of surrealism's most important goals."[19] Artaud observed that film reduced actors to "living signs,"[20] comparable to marionettes, so that a director who was his own writer, cameraman, and editor could really control a multilayered creative process. He can control it in space, since he can create an environment which is entirely his own and which may be held in his hand in the form of a reel of film. He can control it in time, since actions may take just the number of seconds which he decrees, and furthermore when he holds the reel of film he is holding all those seconds at once. The film maker can create a physical universe which is all his own, unhampered by laws of gravity, time, logic. It is worth

19. ". . . une nouvelle sensibilité est en train de naître . . . elle est un des buts les plus importants du surréalisme"—Apollinaire, "Il y a" in *Oeuvres Poétiques,* p. 253. Toward the end of his career Artaud seemed to be turning away from film, however; he called it "a dead art," apparently referring to the impossibility of spontaneity once filming is completed.
20. ". . . signes vivants"—Antonin Artaud, "réponse à une enquête" in *A Propos du Cinéma* in *Oeuvres Complètes* III, p. 74. For a full quotation and discussion, see below, pp. 60, 82.

noting that films are generally judged aesthetically on the basis of their directors' efforts.

Artaud wrote at length about himself and his aesthetic program. Since creation was bound up with the circumstances of an individual artist's momentary state of existence, how the artist had arrived at certain results was of equal interest to the results themselves. Breton and Éluard explained their techniques in great detail, particularly in the *First* and *Second Surrealist Manifestos;* and so did contributors to *SIC* and other surrealist periodicals. Marcel Duchamp's *Green Box* is a collection of the notes he made while creating *The Bride Stripped Bare by her Bachelors, Even (Large Glass)*. Films about film making (Fellini's *8½*, Lester's *How I Won the War*), novels about novel making (Lessing's *The Golden Notebook,* Fowles' *The French Lieutenant's Woman*) are more recent; but their roots are in the surrealist attitude toward creation.

Not only was the role of the artist and his life essential to the surrealist nature of the art work. The surrealist artist and his role were the center of the art work in another sense as well. The twentieth-century artist had new justification for looking to himself as the raw material of art. Psychoanalysis was confirming the intuitions of the romantic tradition of self-expression and inspiration by revealing the psyche as an inexhaustible supply of wonders. To the surrealists these wonders were more real, more surreal, than rational thought can be, especially when they were hallucinatory in style; so surrealist artists tried to tap their psyches.

In order to release his own unconscious, the artist deliberately learned to drug or trick or crush his conscious mind into submission. Artaud did not need to do so, apparently; and other surrealist artists will serve as our examples for the rest of this chapter. Surrealist artists produced work during trances, like Robert Desnos, who learned to enter trances for hours, even in crowded cafés, and to produce streams of poetry or spoken monologues in that state. Breton spoke of phrases "knocking at the window" to be admitted into his consciousness sufficiently to be written down. Breton and Desnos turned out pages of automatic writing, each spate perhaps triggered by a mechanical initial image but thereafter not directed or edited in any way. Apollinaire had been the first to encourage such automatism as the "open sesame"[21] to art. Accusations were sometimes heard in the surrealist ranks that some artist had returned to a finished work in order to disjoint it deliberately, but this we can never prove.

A similar exercise is Breton's and Éluard's experiment in writing as if insane. They wrote *Immaculate Conception* (*L'Immaculée Conception*) in 1930 from the depths of self-induced temporary insanity in an effort to expose a subconscious raging out of rational control.

Perhaps the most free means of transmission for the dictates of the artist's uncontrolled subconscious is the dream. Dreams had been a preoccupation of the late nineteenth century, supported scientifically by Freud whose *On the Interpretation of Dreams* appeared in 1898, and artistically by Gérard de Nerval who actually transcribed dreamed material as literature (*Aurélie*). In fact, by the end of the nineteenth century, "dream . . . stood for a whole . . . mystical tradition in the arts" in Western Europe.[22]

For the surrealists dreams became a full cult of revelation. They were obsessed by dreams as glimpses of, gateways to, and metaphors for the marvelous irrational essence of the universe, accessible to all men. Indeed Breton claimed that the surrealist poet surmounted "the depressing idea of the irreparable divorce between action and dreaming"[23] and described homo sapiens as "this definitive dreamer."[24]

21. Georges Hugnet, quoted in Matthews, *Introduction*, p. 82.
22. Shattuck, *Banquet Years*, pp. 34–35.
23. Breton, *Les Vases Communicants* (1932), quoted in Matthews, *Introduction*, p. 66. The *"Vases"* of Breton's title are the twin states of waking and dreaming.
24. ". . . ce rêveur definitif"—Breton, *First Surrealist Manifesto*, p. 1.

Not only did surrealist writers transcribe their fantasies and reveries; painters, too, used the dream context to work from and also to guide their spectators' responses. Giorgio di Chirico painted arrangements of figures and objects, very solid, but caught in timeless vacuums and in such combinations and positions as to evoke a sensation of nightmare. Hans Arp's compositions of insectlike creatures and Salvador Dali's and René Magritte's more intellectual manipulations of situations (limp watches, a mermaid who is fish above and woman below) were also commonly described as nightmarish.[25]

The dream was an especially inviting form for the surrealists in the theater and ought to be discussed in connection with the surrealist artist himself, as a clue to his creativity. Freud himself had spoken about the dream as a means of "dramatization" of daily life with dream's properties of "spatial" and "sensory" projection.[26] The corollary to this observation is that the theater, appealing to several senses simultaneously, offers a full range of means for acting out a dream. And the merging of life and dream in surrealist ideology, which the surrealists liked to describe by quoting Gérard de Nerval's aphorism that dreams are a "second life," was further invitation to create a stage experience of both states.

The surrealists did not originate the dream play; Strindberg's *A Dream Play* (1902) was the first deliberately realized example of the genre and was, in 1928, the first principal production at Artaud's Théâtre Alfred-Jarry. Calderón (*Life Is a Dream*) and Shakespeare (*A Midsummer Night's Dream*) are among earlier explorers of the dream genre. But almost all surrealist plays utilized to the full the dream's—and the dream play's—external

25. Dali's limp watches are in *The Persistence of Memory* (1935), at the Museum of Modern Art. Magritte's new sort of mermaid is in *L'invention collective* (1931), in the collection of the E. L. T. Mesens in Brussels.

26. Sigmund Freud, *The Interpretation of Dreams*, p. 83. Freud is referring to perceptions of predecessors in the field.

Another nightmare, probably created at least partly through automatic techniques. Yves Tanguy's *A Large Painting which is a Landscape.* Courtesy, William Mozer, New York.

The recurrent motif of birds in Max Ernst's paintings has been said to reflect their importance in his childhood fantasies. *Chaste Joseph* (1928). Oil. Courtesy of M. A. D. Mouradian, Paris.

characteristics: illogic, disregard for laws of time and space, rapid disjointed shifts in action and imagery. The particular highly colored cast of the imagination associated with dreams and dream plays—violent, erotic, mysterious, marvelous, occasionally whimsical—was the atmosphere of surrealist art in general.

Some surrealist plays used dream as did some psychology-oriented expressionist plays (Kaiser's *From Morn to Midnight*, 1912; O'Neill's *The Emperor Jones*, 1920): reality explicated on another level of perception. Yvan Goll's witty *Mathusalem* shows Mathusalem, a pompous unscrupulous potbellied capitalist, falling asleep, whereupon his double, dressed in white, steps out of the mirror and says:

> THE MIRROR: I am You.
> MATHUSALEM: My own Me is good enough.
> THE MIRROR: Know thyself.
>   . . .
>   Rabble! Con man! Thief! Profiteer!

Mathusalem rejects the mirror's advice and threatens it, and it breaks. Then several short films represent his continued dreaming: first he seduces women, then he is part of a performance of *Hamlet*, and then he is a general; each dream scene ends in a triumph for the brand of shoe polish with which he has made his fortune.

However Mathusalem awakens at last and the plot goes on, whereas more purely surrealist plays set up no such rationally simplified correspondences between dream and reality. Surrealism did not accept such constructs, any more than it accepted deliberate games which called reality into question, as in Pirandello's *Six Characters in Search of an Author* (1921). Rather, reality is the material of authentic surrealist dream plays only as the day's waking life is material for the night's dream.

René Daumal's unproduced playlet *en gggarrrde* (1924) is an example of this new sort of dream play. The author appears as a character in the prologue and last scene. He is also identified on the title page as a "good little . . . boy," and a good little boy does, indeed, appear in the epilogue. His appearance in adulthood and childhood simultaneously reinforces the impression that the composite character is the hero of the play and surrogate dreamer of the author's dream. Aside from this one character there is throughout this brief playlet no consistency at all except motion. Certain dreamlike images do recur, however, amid a tone of coy and menacing baby talk: a mushroom sprouting from a head, for example. Someone cries, "Gentlemen, you are the object of an abominable machination. There are strawberries in the world, don't forget!" A comparable non sequitur occurs in action when a group of characters stand on their heads, whereupon a character named The Pernod with Sugar "disappears inside a sea gull, whistling obscenely."

Henri Béhar calls Roger Vitrac's recently discovered play *Free Entry* (whose first English translation appears here) a composite of "authentic dreams."[27] We do not know how faithfully Vitrac transcribed his own dreams. In any case Vitrac uses the dream "as theatrical material." Vitrac had written earlier that he was searching for an instrument for "the utilization of the dramatic power of the dream, and thereby a certain coming-together of life (suddenly total) upon the stage."[28] And in *Free Entry* he seems consciously to confront the dream play as a dramaturgical form and use the "architectures of dreams"[29] as the structure of the play. Instead of presenting its story linearly, and thereby retaining reality as its spine, *Free Entry* uses waking reality merely

---

27. ". . . des rêves authentiques"—Henri Béhar, *Roger Vitrac*, p. 166.
28. ". . . l'utilisation de la puissance dramatique du rêve, et par là une certaine rencontre de la vie (totale cette fois-ci) sur la scène . . ." Vitrac's article "Dormir" in the periodical *Les Hommes du Jour* (Paris, 1923) quoted in Béhar, ibid., p. 77.
29. "Le rêve peut se raconter grâce aux architectures monstrueuses qui ne sont guère que les mots revenus à l'état sauvage." Vitrac in the periodical *Comoedia* (Paris, 1925) quoted by Maguire, p. 270.

as a springboard. *Free Entry* has two sets of three dream-work-
ings of the same story material, arranged around a realistic
scene, so as to reproduce the timelessness of dreams and of surrealist metaphysics. Reality is transmuted into something rich and
strange, which is then fragmented as in dreams. These dream-
scene fragments radiate outward from reality while at the same
time the arrangement of the dream scenes inward around the
realistic Scene Four draws the audience deep into the experience.
One of the characters, Henri, is Vitrac's surrogate dreamer; as
first and last dreamer, he is the primary guide to the dream spectacle and draws the spectator in. But the other two characters,
too, exist as dreaming consciousnesses. By embedding the reality
deep in the center of the play's structure and by refusing to
channel all the dreams totally in the consciousness of a single
character, Vitrac creates the illusion that even the reality scene
is only reality within a dream. The dreamer of that ultimate
dream is not Henri but rather Vitrac himself, or the spectator,
or—compatible with the surrealist doctrine of reconcilation—
Vitrac and the spectator both simultaneously.

An aspect of the significance of the film form to the surrealist
is, in Artaud's words, that the film works through a "dream
mechanism,"[30] and further: "If cinema was not made to translate
dreams or whatever in waking life is related to the domain of
dreams, cinema does not exist."[31] Alain Resnais' much later film
Last Year at Marienbad, which is in many ways directly and
specifically surrealist, is unmistakably dream-like—especially
reminiscent of di Chirico. Stanley Kauffmann speaks of the "clear
. . . dream reality, a surreal *conviction*" from which "the visual
metaphors proceed firmly."[32]

30. ". . . une mécanique de rêve"—Artaud, "La Coquille et le Clergyman,"
in *Oeuvres Complètes* III, p. 77.
31. "Si le cinéma n'est pas fait pour traduire les rêves ou tout ce qui dans la
vie éveillée s'apparente au domaine des rêves, le cinéma n'existe pas."—Artaud,
"La Sorcellerie et Cinéma," in *Oeuvres Complètes* III, p. 81.
32. Stanley Kauffmann, *Figures of Light,* p. 234.

But the surrealists were full of surprises. Paradoxically, surrealism combined the idea of the passionately individual art experience as the key to universal essence with a negation of the individuality of experience. Surrealism asserted the total "equality of all normal human beings before the subliminal message" which is their "common patrimony."[33] All individuals are equally near to and far from the essence of life. Therefore, said Francis Picabia, an individual's pretension to "artistic skill is a mummery that compromises all human dignity,"[34] and the artist's experience is only the experience of an instrument or vehicle.

In that case, all those conscious characteristics which made the artist an individual merely disguised, paradoxically, the psychic forces in him which are universal. So he relinquished his intellect to his subconscious, which was both individual and in a sense collective, and suppressed those external mannerisms which he called his personality or psyche in order to release his inner life which transcended him. Paradoxically, the surrealist not only cultivated his personality but also suppressed and circumvented it in order to reach the universal through the individual. Dreams were thus revelations of both a single inner life and a larger, impersonal, surreality. Had not anthropology taught the mysterious universality of dream images?

As the surrealist relinquished his intellect and will to his subconscious, which was both individual and universal, so he relinquished his will to chance, which was an instrument of surreality. An artist open to chance was allowing the truth to speak to and through him. Apollinaire again was the first to make chance "a powerful ally of poetry."[35] Through art, submitting his conscious rational will to chance or the subconscious or both, the surrealist could approach surreality. The surrealists took to themselves the

33. Breton, quoted in Matthews, *Introduction* . . . , p. 88.
34. Nadeau, *History of Surrealism*, p. 85.
35. George-Emmanuel Clancier, *Rimbaud au Surréalisme*, p. 247.

This pen drawing was made by Man Ray and Yves Tanguy and Joan Miro and Max Morise — all together. *Cadavre Exquis* (1928). Collection of Mr. and Mrs. E. A. Bergman, Chicago, Illinois.

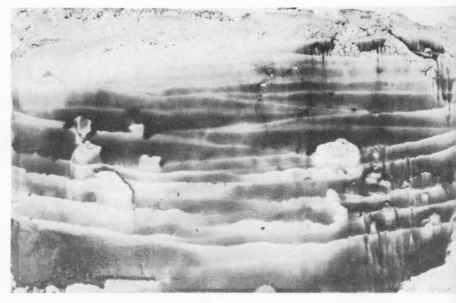

Yves Tanguy, *Decalcomania* (1936). The gouache technique creates the strange effect. Collection, the Museum of Modern Art, New York, Kay Sage Tanguy Fund. Formerly, Marcel Jean Collection. See p. 47.

words of a poem by Apollinaire: "We who still battle at the frontiers/of the infinite and the future. . . ."[36] Beyond the frontiers of "the infinite," the laws of chance and the human psychic forces coincide.

By 1924 the Surrealist movement set up a Bureau of Surrealist Research to conduct experiments with chance and the subconscious. The Bureau's findings were published in the floating surrealist periodicals in solemn scientific form. Parallel with the mission which the surrealists assumed to destroy old categories—social, philosophical, aesthetic—which did not describe the truth, in order to find fresh perceptions of the truth, was their mission to reorganize mistaken conventional distinctions between conscious and unconscious experience.

So we find artists helping art works make themselves. Paul Masson, for example, dusted sand over blobs of glue; when loose sand blew off, patterns remained, and these he called his finished work. Marcel Duchamp and Man Ray used machine action to create images. Frottage and decalcomania were other techniques which depended solely on chance for the visual effects they produced.

So, too, we find groups of artists and dilettantes solemnly playing word games. Each player contributed a word to a poem without knowing the others' contributions, for example; or wildly disparate clauses beginning "if" and "when" were jammed together. The results were nonsense which, however, occasionally contained startling images and strange appeals to something dimly sensed below the surface of the words. Reverdy called these "sparks" which were struck by a simple "coming-together which is to some extent fortuitous."[37] Apollinaire's poem "The

36.   Nous qui combattons toujours aux frontières
        De l'illimité et de l'avenir . . .
Apollinaire, "La Jolie Rousse" in *Il Y A* in *Oeuvres Complètes*, p. 313.
37. ". . . rapprochement en quelque sorte fortuit"—Matthews, *Introduction*, p. 105.

Windows" was supposedly composed by the poet and some friends sitting around a café table and taking turns, line by line. Art works produced by such processes do not have single creators. However they do emerge from a common experience as well as, theoretically, from a mystical essence common to all individuals. In the theater, the art work was of necessity partially dependent on chance. Even rehearsed plays change nightly because they are experienced afresh each time. Furthermore, for the earliest Dada and surrealist soirées at the Cabaret Voltaire and in Parisian halls, the audiences' reactions were violently unpredictable; they shaped the theater events, and plans for the events included this variability and potential chaos. Performances without scripts or rehearsed performers, or with performers free to choose on the spot among alternative sequences of actions—prototypes of the Happenings of the 1960s—carried the principle still further.

For surrealism, spontaneity is the keyword to all aspects and techniques of creating an art work. There are to be no barriers between the artist's self and what he produces. "Thought is made in the mouth."[38] "Painting is made in the hand."[39] Dreaming, automatic writing, game playing—all these reject rational planning of form and content in favor of a free extension of the artist's life into art. Action paintings (and the Happenings which came after) are simply instantaneous materializations of the artist's spontaneous act. In the next chapter we will follow the artist and his action into the creation itself: the nature of the art work which he produced.

---

38. "La pensée se fait dans la bouche."—Tzara, "Le Manifeste sur l'amour faible et l'amour amer" (1920) in *Lampisteries*, p. 58.
39. "La peinture se fait dans la main."—Tzara, *Picasso et les chemins de la connaissance.*

CHAPTER FOUR

Surrealist Art

In 1925 a group of young surrealists tried to establish a Théâtre de la Tour Eiffel on the Tower's lower landing. They prepared an evening of, in Breton's phrase, "black comedy" sketches for the opening but in the end were refused permission to rent the space. Nevertheless we might say that all surrealist art created the same heady atmosphere that might have been present in a theater on the landing of the Eiffel Tower.

We saw in Chapter Two that surrealist life and philosophy were concentrated in surrealist art and by means of it. In Chapter Three we saw that surrealist art was concentrated in the artist and was a natural expression of his surrealist self. In the final chapter we will see that the audience, too, had to be drawn into the artist's identity—"reconciled" with him—by means of their common art experience. In this chapter we will examine the characteristics of the art works themselves which put artist and audience in touch with surreality.

As the romantic tendency had always been, surrealist artists worked in traditional forms, which they shaped to their distinctive own uses. Surrealist philosophy bore very directly on surrealist art theories.

Surrealism's joyous embracing of chaos, for example, naturally made alien all classical structure. All art works had to reflect the universal dissolution of structure. Besides, formal patterns were impossible if art works were to emerge as the artist's spontaneous experiences. Finally, the distinction between content and treatment, which implies an orderly intellectual approach to creation, was discredited with all other theoretical distinctions, for pure nonrationality could not admit of it.

For all these reasons, association and repetition took the place of structure in surrealist literature and drama; in the latter, of course, the Aristotelian unities, with complications and denouement and characters behaving consistently, were obviously unacceptable to the surrealists. The characteristic extreme brevity of surrealist poems and plays and (Satie's) music made the shape imposed on them by their beginnings and ends seem to serve as structure. Art forms which seem to require a certain intellectual coherence and sustained control, such as the novel or the symphony, were rarely attempted by the surrealists; Breton's novel *Nadja* is an exception.

The universal nonrational chaos which the surrealists perceived led them to dismiss, along with structure, all rational distinctions but one: "my experience"—itself a nonrational entity—versus everything else (according to Freud, the infant's first distinction);[1] and even this distinction dissolved at the level of surreality. The perception of general disintegration confirmed their concentration of all things and ideas in the individual experience. It also inevitably made all their art works chaotic as well.

We saw how all surrealist art experience was centered in the artist. In other words mimesis, or imitation, of the world around the artist, the traditional goal of all the arts, was no longer tenable for the surrealists. Indeed mimesis as a goal of art seemed particularly absurd with the dissolution of confidence in the accuracy of mental and sensory perceptions, in the possibility of communicating such perceptions without distortion, and, finally,

---

1. Sigmund Freud, *Civilization and Its Discontents*, pp. 13–15.

in the unlikelihood that the recipient's impression will ever be what you intended. It seemed impossible even to discover what that final impression was. Again, the absence of faith in rationality, the adoption in its place of nonrationality, is the prime motif in surrealist art.

In rejecting mimesis, surrealist art was firmly in the nineteenth-century line of development which put the artist, rather than imitation of an external subject, at the center of the art work. At the same time as the artist was coming to be popularly considered a special creature deserving honor for his role and life style as well as for the art works he produces, he was also attaining a kind of semi-divinity for his ability literally to create worlds according to his will. The surrealist self-image in life and art clearly fits this general pattern.

In nineteenth-century painting, for example, the picture was released from the tyranny of subject. We begin to trace, along with a continuing stream of Academy painters, a movement from the Impressionists, who applied their individual personalities to a landscape and simultaneously used the landscape to express their personalities, and culminating in Cézanne who went so far as actually to deform the landscape for the sake of the picture.

Another way of describing this tendency away from imitation is to say that art was not serving the artist's environment. It no longer aimed automatically to reflect the environment, realistically or symbolically; nor to elucidate it; nor to effect its social reform or spiritual uplift in the usual senses; nor simply to decorate it. All these traditional goals seemed particularly hopeless with the dissolution of confidence in the accuracy of mental and sensory perceptions, as well as in the possibility of communicating such perceptions to others rationally so that they may perceive them in exactly the same way. Instead, environment was at the service of art and the artist; and surrealist art and artists, of course, were at the service of higher spiritual values.

The surrealists were not drawn by those art forms too inher-

ently mimetic for reshaping. Novels, for example, have traditionally been mimetic, involving a subject which is, in Henry James's
words, a "direct impression or perception of life."[2] "Impression"
presupposes the possibility of rationally communicating such an
impression, and indeed the surrealists wrote very few novels. Perhaps the only real one, in fact, was *Nadja* by André Breton, which
we have just mentioned. A free series of encounters between the
author and a woman (apparently surrealist in life style) who is
probably based on an acquaintance of the author's, it avoids
imitating a real-life story as plot. This is quite different from the
contemporaneous Joycean stream of consciousness, which imi-
tates fictional minds reacting to an objective environment beneath
a series of rational events—all presented so that the reader can
even follow chronologically. Forty years later, novelists Marguer-
ite Duras and Alain Robbe-Grillet seem to be wrestling to create
nonmimetic novels, and they are both drawn to writing for films;
Beckett (*Watt, Malone*) has probably come the closest to achieving that goal. Such novels are collages of passages of meticu-
lously observed mimetic writing, put together so as to reflect
nothing at all. In painting they resemble, for example, Magritte's
close reproductions of impossibly juxtaposed objects.

Music ought perhaps to be the perfect surrealist form. Walter
Sokel observes that whereas sculpture, with its imitation of natural forms, had always been the prototypical art of the West,
music was now taking over: "the adoption of . . . principles of
musical composition by the other arts is probably the single most
dominant characteristic of all modernism."[3] Surrealism was of

2. Henry James, *The Art of the Novel* (New York: Charles Scribner's Sons,
1962), p. 45.
3. Sokel, *Writer in Extremis*, p. 26. Also, on the connection of a society's
technology and music, see Crombie, *Science in the West.*
Pater, of course, had pronounced (in "The School of Giorgione" in *Studies
in the History of the Renaissance*) that "art constantly aspires to the condition
of music."

course an expression of modernity. Music refers solely to the universe of the individual art experience. The conventional distinction between content and form cannot be applied to it. Music's unsuitability to function as a vehicle of intellection and its property of seeming to touch universals which elude logical verbalization seem to confirm surrealism's affinity with it. It is also possible to argue that musicalization occurred as men learned to manipulate abstractions and, in particular, to apply them to everyday life—as an aspect, in other words, of technological development.

Nevertheless, the Surrealist movement produced very little music. Erik Satie was the only well-known musician to be officially linked with the movement, although some of his disciples, Les Six (especially Auric, Poulenc, Milhaud, Tailleferre), occasionally contributed compositions to Dada or surrealist soirées, as did also Stravinsky. Aristotle called music the most mimetic of all arts, although he meant imitation of emotional states rather than of ideas or objective impressions. Perhaps music was prevented from conveying the artist's transformation from imitator to creator by the fact that it is a self-contained artificial universe which does not refer at all to its environment, and because it is purely sensory. Certainly rationality and irrationality are adjectives which are difficult to apply to music. Furthermore, music, like theater, requires performers to complete creatively the composer's creative impulse. Much of Satie's music is for solo piano, and the pianist was usually Satie himself. Indeed Satie's techniques approach music very much as surrealist artists in other media approached painting and other conventional forms, and the parallel will reappear.

On the other hand, the surrealists were drawn to those traditional art forms which could be practiced in nonstructured nonmimetic ways. Lyric poetry, for example, as a free expression of the poet's feelings, was very congenial to the surrealists, almost all of whom wrote poems, at least sometimes, to express a love or a mood. What was different about some surrealist poetry was the kind of language in which it was written; but that we will discuss when we look at absolutely surrealist inventions.

Surrealist painting, especially when it was the product of automatism, was sometimes purely nonmimetic. More often it was actively antimimetic. The surrealists used the art form to play with viewers' expectations of imitation; they reproduced certain features of the external world, but in unexpected, arresting arrangements which come from the artist and not from his impressions of the world. Surrealist paintings were cerebral rather than sensory, almost literary, almost verbal, so it was this arrangement of pictured objects and creatures rather than a retreat to abstractions in pure color or design which constituted surrealist nonmimetic tendencies in painting.[4]

Similarly, surrealist sculptures, for the most part, neither represented human beings, nor distorted them according to a program. Rather they tended to be constructions: a whole new form, which we will discuss at greater length later, made of recognizable bits of the physical environment so combined as to stymie any attempt to correlate these bits rationally with that environment. They also differed from tradition in that they were rarely pleasing to the senses in design or texture.

Early surrealist experiments with film mostly avoided the abstract exercises in design and color—"pure film"—which were popular among other contemporary film makers, in favor of film-

4. There were two approximately contemporary schools of painting which surrealism especially resembled in attitude toward mimesis. One was the fauvists (around 1905), who freed themselves from imitation to provide joyous sensual release through color. The other was the cubists (around 1910), who distorted shapes for the intellectual pleasure of seeing them differently and surprisingly: for seeing *through* them in a "quest for the essence of things" which would be tapped to flow in a "mysterious current from the artist straight to the spectator's soul." The cubists also tried to cut across or compress time. It is not irrelevant that Apollinaire was the cubists' earliest critical champion.

It is the juxtaposition of the cabbages and other solid images that makes them striking. Giorgio de Chirico, *The Philosopher's Conquest* (1914). Oil. Courtesy of the Art Institute of Chicago, the Joseph Winterbottom Collection.

Starfish in jars proliferate in Man Ray's film of Desnos' play *L'Étoile de Mer.*
Note the hand among the other objects. Permission, Cinémathèque Française,
Paris. See p. 57.

ing recognizable places or things but defying the spectator to construe the film as imitation of anything. In surrealist film, as much as possible, said a practitioner: "the story is nothing, but the vision is everything . . .": ". . . shadows and lights and their possibilities. . . ."[5] Avant-garde French and Italian films of the last ten years seem to be following his dictum.

In drama the drive away from mimesis—from the story—impelled surrealist philosophy actually to fight the art form itself. Ever since Aristotle's *Poetics* named mimesis as the basis of tragedy, drama's conscious source has been imitation of life. The traditional ingredients of dramatic form integrally involve imitation of life and of lifelike thinking processes: characters with some psychological consistency; plots with some cause-and-effect logic progressing in time; and dialogue with some functional plausibility. All these were antithetical to surrealism, which thought of them, in Eugene O'Neill's contemptuous phrase of the same period, as merely "holding the family kodak up to nature."[6]

Not surprisingly, two extreme categories of plays emerged from Dada and surrealism, according to the dramatists' attitudes toward retention of mimesis: one sort which was not really surrealistic, and another which was not really drama. Some playwrights of the first category simply violated surrealist principles. The art form here was too strong for the abstract principles. Many surrealist plays have traceable plots, and most of these even progress chronologically, if obscurely. Even when this progression is not logical, a story nevertheless seems to be unrolling on the stage, in the telling of which a time sequence is basically

5. "Dans le film, l'histoire n'est rien, mais la vision est tout . . . on devrait étudier les complémentaires oppositoires des ombres et lumières et leurs possibilités de provoquer des correspondances voulues ou imprévues dans le domaine imaginaire et spirituel."—Raoul Haussmann in Kyrou, *Surréalisme au Cinéma*, p. 172.

6. Eugene O'Neill, "Strindberg and our Theatre," in *American Playwrights on Drama*, edited by Horst Frenz (New York: Hill and Wang, 1965), p. 2.

honored. And the characters in the story have some recognizable
consistency.

It is true that, usually, even the plays which are dramaturgically most mimetic do exemplify surrealist life values and their
dialogue resembles surrealist poetry. An example is *The Emperor
of China* by Dadaist Georges Ribemont-Dessaignes, in which
royal characters die violently after an incestuous love. Nevertheless the familiar material of domestic drama and conventional
romance is not far off. Vitrac's play *The Mysteries of Love* shows
us the violent relationship between two lovers, Patrice and Léa;
Tzara's *Cloud Handkerchief* is about a poet who has an affair
with a banker's wife and later kills himself; Desnos' charming *La
Place de l'Étoile* is about a young man and two women who perhaps love him; Apollinaire's *Sky Blue* is about three young space-
ship adventurers who find their ideal embodied in a woman and
destroy themselves over her; Neveux's *Juliette or the Key to
Dreams* is about a young man who goes hunting for his once-
glimpsed love; Goll's *Mathusalem* is about the marriage between
a romantic middle-class girl (Mathusalem's daughter) and a revolutionary on the make; Aragon's *The Mirror Wardrobe One Fine
Evening* is about a jealous husband.

The other extreme category of surrealist playwrights followed
their principles right out of the theater. Clément Pansaers' *The
Smack-smack on the Naked Negro's Ass*, with no action at all of
any sort and no characters, is written in a sort of automatic-
writing prose rather than dialogue. Roger Gilbert-Lecomte's *The
Odyssey of Ulysses the Palimped*, with no plot or interacting
characters, calls for a range of activities which defy staging.
These are pieces to be read silently, as one reads a poem; Armand
Salacrou actually called his *A Circus Story* a "play for reading."
Like Gertrude Stein's contemporaneous *Turkey and Bones and
Eating* and others, such plays have given up all connection with
stage, performance, audience. Plays in name only, they are no

longer drama and probably no longer theater events. Nevertheless, Tristan Tzara's *The Gas Heart*—three acts of repetitive nonsense inexplicably spoken by Nose, Ear, Neck, and other facial parts—did indeed give satisfaction of some sort when produced, as has Kenneth Koch's much more recent but similar effort *Bertha.*

The majority of surrealist playwrights compromised, retaining a story about certain characters but making it a dream-play of shifts, surprises, nonsense, violence, and laughter. "When man wanted to imitate walking," Apollinaire said in his Preface to *The Breasts of Tiresias,* "he created the wheel, which does not resemble a leg. In the same way he has created surrealism without knowing it."[7] The surrealist version of conventional mimetic drama, with flexibility and verve, was intended to be to most plays as the wheel is to the leg: a better, more genuine way to do the same thing. In *La Place de L'Étoile,* starfish proliferate delightfully; throughout the second act characters talk about them: "salty, fat, fresh from the sea." Vitrac's *The Painter* begins with a surrealist imitation of an action: the action is surrealist in itself, and the imitation remains not quite a plot.

(. . . *A painter is painting a door red. Enter a small boy carefully dressed in white. He approaches the painter and watches him painting.*)

PAINTER:	What's your name?
CHILD:	Maurice Parchment. (*Silence.*) And yours?
PAINTER:	That's my name too.
LITTLE MAURICE PARCHMENT:	It's not true.
PAINTER:	It's not true? (*Silence.*) You're right.

7. "Quand l'homme a voulu imiter la marche, il a créé la roue qui ne ressemble pas à une jambe. Il a fait ainsi du surréalisme sans le savoir." Apollinaire, Préface to *Les Mamelles de Tirésias* (*The Breasts of Tiresias*), in *Oeuvres Poétiques,* pp. 865–66.

(*He paints the child's face red.* LITTLE MAURICE PARCHMENT *goes out crying . . . The* PAINTER *goes on painting. Enter* MADAME PARCHMENT *. . . and little* MAURICE PARCHMENT, *cleaned up.*)

MME. PARCHMENT: Sir, you are contemptible. What is your name?

PAINTER: Maurice Parchment.

MME. PARCHMENT: It's not true.

PAINTER: It's not true? (*Silence.*) You are right.

(*He paints their faces red.* MME. PARCHMENT *and little* MAURICE PARCHMENT *go out crying. The* PAINTER *goes on painting. . . .*) [Much later in the action he will inexplicably look in the mirror, paint his own face red, and exit crying. Note, by the way, the pun; parchment is to be painted on.]

The compromise between the rejection of mimesis and the retention of dramaturgical conventions is similar to the effort to synthesize a "universal athlete" to produce an entire theater piece all by himself. Perhaps the tensions involved in such conflicts between the demand of form, of practice, and of aesthetic theory are responsible at least in part for the energy inherent in surrealist drama.

The surrealist ideal in drama had in fact been summed up in the Prologue to *The Breasts of Tiresias:*

> . . . the theatre should not be a copy of reality
> It is right that the dramatist should use
> All the mirages at his disposal. . . .
> It is right that he should let crowds speak
>   inanimate objects
> If he so pleases
> And that he no longer should reckon with time
> Or space
> His universe is the play
> Within which he is God the Creator
> Who disposes at will
> Of sounds gestures movements masses colors

Men running, a path, trees are all startlingly juxtaposed at this instant of the film *Entr'acte*. Permission, Cinémathèque Française, Paris.

A scene from Ribemont-Dessaignes' play *L'Empereur de Chine,* as presented at the Autant-Lara Théâtre de l'Art et Action. Photo courtesy of Annabelle Henkin.

Not merely in order
To photograph what is called a slice of life
But to bring forth life itself in all its truth. . . .

In practice, of course, it was difficult to accomplish all this on a stage.

One weapon against dramatic mimesis was sabotage of stage illusion. It was a Frenchman, Zola, who in the late nineteenth century called for a theater of perfectly reproduced naturalistic "slices of life." It was another Frenchman, Diderot, who in the mid-eighteenth century had described the perfect theatrical imitation of life as giving the illusion that one is looking into a real household's activities through its transparent fourth wall: the proscenium. Ever since Albert-Birot's *théâtre nunique*, projected in 1917, the French surrealists were intent on destroying that wall. The *théâtre nunique* had several revolving concentric circles for performers and audience.[8] Similarly, Tzara's *Cloud Handkerchief* actually showed the actors making up in onstage dressing rooms and commenting on the play. In 1923 Kurt Schwitters began to sketch a Normalbühne Merz "for which he conceived a space stage in which the machinery constituted part of the visible aesthetic of the event."[9]

Actors in surrealist stage plays did not attempt to believe a role in any sense nor to give audiences the illusion of the role's reality. In the 1960s Michael Kirby discussed this new kind of acting in connection with Happenings.[10] He contrasted actors working from mimetic "matrices" of time-place-character with "nonmatrixed" actors like the Living Theater and Jerzy Grotowski's Polish Laboratory Theater, who are closer to dancers than to conventional actors, especially perhaps to dancers of such currently avant-garde dance groups as Merce Cunningham's. Es-

---

8. *SIC*, Nos. 21–22 (September–October, 1917), n.p.
9. William S. Rubin, *Dada, Surrealism, and Their Heritage*, p. 60.
10. Michael Kirby, *Happenings*, p. 15.

pecially in movies, where he was a marionette or "living sign" for the director, the actor's art lay for the surrealists in self-dramatization, as did the art of artists in other media. The pure power of presence, rather than impersonation, was the actor's gift. As we have already noted, Breton had a horror of role-playing.

Antonin Artaud's *Jet of Blood* and his scenarios give us a clue to the surrealist ideal in drama and are perhaps further evidence that the cinema was born with surrealism to be surrealism's element. The world which a film maker can create can be inconsistent beyond fantasy, beyond anthropomorphism. And since the audience sees not actions but pictures of actions, the mimetic illusion of reality is perhaps even less encouraged than onstage.

So the surrealists played with the usual arts. But in the process, their verve pushed and spilled out of the standard containers and was, as was fashionable for furniture at the time, "free form."

Language itself was escaping from old forms. "O mouths," the surrealists exulted, "man is in search of a new language/Which won't be the business of any grammarian in any tongue."[11] For since neither logical thought nor orderly systems of expression seemed tenable any longer, language for the surrealists had lost its value as a vehicle of articulation. Rather, language was to serve, if at all, as a means of touching and sharing surreality.

We ought to get a sense of this language of chaos even before we enter the world of purely surrealist art forms, because all the surrealist arts are in a sense literary. Surrealism has been described as, simply, "a literary school," despite the presence of so many painters and sculptors as members. The movement's principal sources and founders were writers: Jarry and Apollinaire, Tzara (who remained faithful to Dada), Breton, Éluard, Aragon,

11. Raymond Nacenta, "Préface" in *Le surréalisme—sources—histoire—affinités*, n.p.

Simple pictures and simple words combine with unexpectedly complex effect.
The title of this painting was a familiar surrealist phrase. René Magritte, *La Clef
des Songes (The Key of Dreams)*. Oil. Collection of Jasper Johns, New York.

This "collage poem," as Breton called it, is a collage of both things and poetry. André Breton, *Pour Jacqueline* (1937). Collection of Mr. and Mrs. E. A. Bergman, Chicago, Illinois. See p. 67.

and Soupault. Many of its members who were not primarily writers acknowledged their personal inspiration to have been literary in origin. Duchamp, for example, called Roussel's dramatized novel *Impressions of Africa* the greatest single influence on his work. (Apollinaire had taken him to see it.) Indeed Duchamp described surrealist painting in general as "intimately and consciously involved with literature."[12] The surrealists expressed themselves collectively and individually through constantly issued manifestos, through speeches, and through a series of small literary magazines with picturesque names, such as *SIC, Littérature, La Révolution Surréaliste* (later to become the communist *Le Surréalisme au Service de la Révolution*), *Minotaure, Cannibale,* and *L'Oeuf dur* (Hard-Boiled Egg). This pervasive literary-ness may well be related to the movement's cerebral rather than sensual atmosphere and its origin in verbalized philosophical ideas.

Already in the nineteenth century Rimbaud had attempted to separate words from their intellectual functions and conventional meanings. His *Les Illuminations (Illuminations)* had tried to develop a language which would be truly "from the soul to the soul."[13] Then Mallarmé, whom the surrealists often quoted (and who had championed the first scandalous performance of *King Ubu*), further liberated words from their conventional senses. Enormously influential in modern European literature, Mallarmé distinguished between "immediate speech"—for the rational uses of everyday existence—and "essential speech"—to deal with the essence of things. (This is reminiscent of Kant's distinction between the "logical" and "aesthetic" attributes of language and of the more familiar perception which Cocteau formulated as "poetry *in* the theater" versus "poetry *of* the theater"—which is

---

12. Marcel Duchamp, *Marchand du Sel*, p. 112.
13. ". . . une langue qui serait véritablement de l'âme pour l'âme. . . ."—Raymond Nacenta, "Préface" in *Le surréalisme—sources—histoire—affinités*, n.p.

beyond words).[14] Mallarmé attempted to use words and syllables, free of "worn-out, rational meanings,"[15] to give "a purer sense to the words of the tribe"[16] and to affect readers in a nonrational way. He attempted consciously to use language in poetry as composers use sound in music, and not for sound alone but, in Peacock's dramaturgical term, as "emotional metaphors."[17]

Because of their philosophy, which negated the concept of rationality and led them systematically to destroy the sense behind groups of words (as well as behind visual images in paintings and behind series of behavioral gestures), Dada and the surrealists were naturally among Mallarmé's principal heirs. They were "renouncing a devastated language made impossible by journalism" in order to "withdraw into the most profound alchemy of the word."[18] Breton proclaimed some time later that "the words have stopped playing; the words are making love";[19] the surrealist poet "had put his hand on the primary material (in the alchemistic sense) of language."[20] By sound and sight, the liberated words were to evoke reactions from the subconscious, vestigially primitive soul of the reader or listener. For doing so, as for tapping a universal essence, they were much more effectual than conventional sense. They had "a great power for setting off fires."[21] As Artaud said of Seneca's tragedies: "In Seneca pri-

14. Cocteau, Introduction to *The Wedding on the Eiffel Tower* in *Théâtre,* p. 45.
15. Lemaître, *Cubism to Surrealism,* p. 204.
16. ". . . un sens plus pur aux mots de la tribu."—"Le Tombeau d'Edgar Allan Poe" in Stéphane Mallarmé, *Oeuvres Complètes de Stéphane Mallarmé,* p. 70.
17. Ronald Peacock, *The Art of Drama,* p. 52 and throughout.
18. Hugo Ball, *Flucht aus der Zeit* (1927), quoted in Matthews, *Introduction* . . . , p. 23.
19. "Les mots ont fini de jouer. Les mots font l'amour."—Breton, *Les pas perdus,* p. 17.
20. ". . . avait mis la main sur la matière première (au sens alchimique) de la langue."—Nacenta, n.p.
21. ". . . ces mots . . . ont un grand pouvoir de déflagration."—Béhar, *Étude sur le Théâtre Dada et Surréaliste,* p. 158.

mordial forces make their echo heard in the spasmodic vibration of the words."[22]

From these words the surrealists made a musicalized poetry. By 1916 Hugo Ball, the Dadaist, was writing phonetic poems, strings of syllables. At the Café Voltaire, Dada's first home in Zurich, these phonetic poems provided the material for formal theatrical performances. On one occasion, Ball, costumed as an obelisk, recited "slowly and majestically" such lines as "gadgi beri bimba glandridi laula lonni cadori" and moved his body rhythmically.[23] Occasionally Tzara performed "simultaneous poems" with Richard Huelsenbeck and Marcel Janco. This "contrapuntal recitative" included whistling, sirens, and wails. *SIC* published phonetic poetry, sometimes in several voice parts printed in vertical strips side by side as if sounding simultaneously, evoking train or ship or other inhuman noises.

The power of these poems came less from their intellectual freight than from the "poetic radiations emanating from their syllables."[24] Like incantations they stirred irrational feelings. Strange subliminal effects were the goal, whether the words were dictated by chance or by the subconscious. Sometimes even the most elementary word unity broke down into incantation. Hugo Ball's phonetic poetry consisted of nonsense syllables and exotic proper names. So did the dialogue of Tzara's early play *The First Heavenly Adventure of Mr. Aspirin.*

Again we must connect a surrealist characteristic with a characteristic of cinema. Pierre Albert-Birot had written in *SIC* as early as 1919 that (silent) cinema was particularly suited for permitting artists "to realize . . . a great number of surreali-

---

22. "Dans Sénèque les forces primordiales font entendre leur écho dans la vibration spasmodique des mots. Et les noms qui désignent des secrets et des forces les désignent dans le trajet de ces forces et avec leur force d'arrachement et de broiement."—Artaud, letter to Jean Paulhan (1932), in *Oeuvres Complétès* III, p. 304.

23. Richter, *Dada,* p. 42.

24. Lemaître, *From Cubism to Surrealism,* p. 86.

ties."[25] Indeed Artaud preferred silent films even after talkies became popular. He wrote in the preface to *The Shell and the Clergyman* (his only produced scenario) that cinema bypasses words to use "an inorganic language which moves the spirit by osmosis and with no kind of transposition in the words."[26] Artaud believed in using language only to combine and heighten action: "make the images bounce back"[27] as in his scenario *The Butcher's Revolt,* in which the rare spoken phrases have enormous power.

But really, to shift briefly from a historical perspective to a critical one, we might say that surrealist poems, paintings, even plays, seem effective now only in the ways that poems-paintings-plays have traditionally made their effects; their surrealist characteristics seem a relative stylistic distinction like any other. The surrealists only seem to come stunningly into their own when their ideas explode into entirely new forms, like unearthly seeds inexorably surfacing as never-before-seen flowers: new colors, new shapes and unpredictable sizes, new perfumes. These are the art forms of disintegration and chaos.

With the disintegration of logical thinking and articulation came disintegration of all the commonsense distinctions which are the basis of rational communication and traditional art. Perhaps the most basic conventional distinction to disappear was that between life and art. As we have seen in other connections all along, the surrealists considered art different from life in degree rather than in kind. In *The Wedding on the Eiffel Tower,* The Dealer in Modern Paintings tries to sell to the Collector of Modern Paintings the live ongoing wedding party, which he calls

---

25. ". . . réaliser . . . un grand nombre de surréalités."—Albert-Birot, "Du Cinéma" in *SIC* (Nos. 49–50, October 15 and 30, 1919), n.p.

26. ". . . un langage inorganique qui émeut l'esprit par osmose et sans aucune espèce de transposition dans les mots."—Artaud, in *Oeuvres Complètes* III, p. 23.

27. ". . . faire rebondir les images . . ."—Artaud, *La Révolte du Boucher,* in *Oeuvres Complètes* III, p. 47.

One of the earliest ready mades, or assemblages of found objects. Marcel Duchamp's original *Bicycle Wheel* (1913) is lost; this is a third version (1951). Collection, the Museum of Modern Art, New York. Sidney and Harriet Janis Collection.

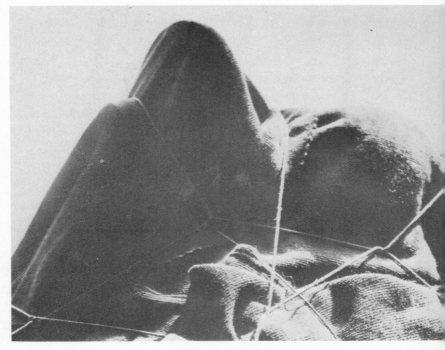

Man Ray constructed this out of cloth and rope over a sewing machine and called it *The Enigma of Isidore Ducasse*. The original (1920) has disappeared; this is the Museum of Modern Art's replica, reproduced here by Man Ray's permission. Collection, the Museum of Modern Art, New York.

"a truly unique piece" entitled "The Wedding Party": "a kind of primitive," "one of the latest works of God," unsigned because "God does not sign" but ". . . look at that paint! What texture!" The Collector makes a deal and a large placard SOLD is propped against the merrymakers, who pay no attention. Their existence is art by arbitrary definition.

Thus an artist might find an art work entirely "ready-made" for him by his environment, simply waiting to be called an art work. Marcel Duchamp defined a ready-made, in fact, as "a usual object promoted to the dignity of art object by the simple choice of the artist."[28] Perhaps the best-known example of this genre is the urinal which he displayed, upside down, at the New York Independents' Exhibition of 1917, entitled blandly "Fountain." Satie used bits of popular tunes in his compositions. Apollinaire used snatches of overheard conversations in his poems. Noise music, originated by the Italian Futurists but adopted by the Surrealists, consisted of machine noises, falling objects, and so on; Hugo Ball composed a complete "Noise music concert" and conducted it behind a screen at the Café Voltaire.

Sometimes Duchamp even allowed the environment to continue to operate in forming the art work. As a wedding gift for his sister, he fastened a book, open, on the balcony of her apartment and allowed the wind and rain to alter and finally demolish the pages. Nature and chance participated in creation. The construction was entitled "Readymade Triste" ("Sad Readymade"), and it held its identity as an art work until it finally disappeared.

The dissolution of distinctions between life and art helps explain a phenomenon which we have already observed in connection with the surrealist artist's life style: "gestures" or "manifestations" of behavior were equivalent to art works. They

28. ". . . un objet usuel promu à la dignité d'objet d'art par le simple choix de l'artiste."—Katharine S. Dreier and Matta Echaurren, *Duchamp's Glass.*

were a sort of "readymade" in the medium of action. The merging of life and art also led to a kind of theatricalization of art. Action paintings, for example, offer for the spectator's view the action as well as the canvas—the verb "painting" as well as the noun; and the burgeoning of art works into Environments (as we shall see) and later into Happenings is another aspect of the same attitude. This refusal to differentiate between life and art is reflected in pop art's reproductions of soup cans and comic strips.

The cabaret soirée, a Dada and surrealist institution which we have had occasion to mention, can serve us now as an example of the way Dada and surrealist life and art reflected their world view of nonrational chaos. It was, in a way, the surrealist art form par excellence. It was also closer to theater than to any other single conventional category.

First of all, the soirée was both social and artistic in intent; Surrealism had after all abolished the distinction between these two spheres. It was a social occasion in the course of which art works were informally performed and exhibited. As in theory it was impossible to separate life and art, so it is impossible to isolate the art works which formed part of any soirée from their social context. Soirées were parties of friends and friendly enemies. Displaying and appreciating flamboyant behavior, greeting friends, eating and drinking—all were equally part of the experience, along with entertainment to be performed or watched with varying degrees of seriousness. Outsiders sometimes appeared at soirées, especially at those held in theaters or hired halls, and their presence added another amusing element.

At soirées, the conventional distinction between performers and audience was loose and shifting, since they were literally a single unified group of participants. They interchanged roles fluidly, acting and reacting. The spatial arrangement of the café floor encouraged this fluidity and influenced the surrealist theater

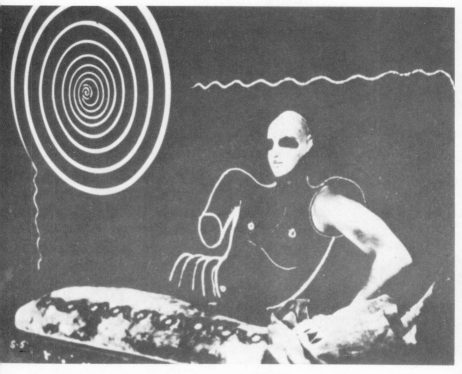

The media which Jean Cocteau mixes dramatically here are painting, sculpture, and a human arm — all shown on film. From *Blood of a Poet*. Collection, the Museum of Modern Art, New York, Film Archive.

Apollinaire's "Poème du 9 février 1915." The calligramme in the top left corner begins: "I look at myself in this mirror and see you, my Lou..." The lady's hatbrim in the bottom left corner says: "This adorable person is you." The other calligrammes which make up the poem are a cannonball, a monument, a sabre, and an orange; Apollinaire wrote them from the trenches for his mistress Lou. In *Poèmes à Lou*, reprinted by permission of Éditions Gallimard, Paris. See p. 68.

experiments in which, as we have seen, the proscenium dissolves and stage and hall become confused. In Tzara's play *The Gas Heart,* presented as part of a soirée, there was even a speaker stationed over the audience's heads, facing the stage, and occasionally making on their behalf such blasé comments as "It's charming, your play, but one can't understand a word of it."

With the acceptance of chaos, the collage, which was not a new form, now gained the status of art. The soirée was a sort of collage of life situations. Bits of materials of all sorts—visual, verbal, and dramatic—combined in no perceptive pattern, reflected a universe arranged in the same way. Breton observed that collages assembled by chance "offer insight into a world where the distinction between necessity and accident had been lost."[29]

The surrealists also repudiated formal distinctions between genres, which seemed to them no more valid than those between life and art or between waking consciousness and dreams. The soirée was a collage of art forms, too. It was composed of many parts, often haphazardly arranged. A Dada-Surrealist soirée entitled "Le Coeur à Barbe" ("The Bearded Heart"), held in Paris in 1923, included a brilliant variety of offerings in an environment designed for the occasion. The program included: films by Man Ray, Charles Cheeler, Paul Strand; poems by Cocteau, Tzara, Éluard, Zdanevitch, Soupault; musical compositions by Stravinsky, Milhaud, Auric; dances by Lizica Codreanu. It also included plays by Tzara and Ribemont-Dessaignes, which were in turn composed of poetry, acting, decor, costumes, dance.

Mixing of media was typical of surrealist art activities even outside the soirée. Apollinaire combined language and visual arts in witty poems arranged to form appropriate pictures in type: a mandolin, a necktie, stripes of falling raindrops.[30] This was a

---

29. Matthews, *Introduction* . . . , p. 105.
30. Apollinaire, "La Mandoline L'Oeillet et le Bambou" in *Étendards* in *Oeuvres Poétiques*, p. 209. "La Cravate et la Montre" and "Il pleut" in *Calligrammes*, ibid., pp. 192, 203.

popular seventeenth-century device which he adopted and named calligrammes; a recently fashionable name for it is "concrete poetry." Tzara included typographical decorations in the printing of his play *The Gas Heart*. Satie decorated his scores with marginal cartoons and clever comments. The Satie-Picabia ballet *Relâche* included a short film by René Clair, showing, among other scenes, Satie firing a cannon on a roof. Magritte wrote, "This is not a pipe" across the canvas of his straightforward painting of a pipe, whose original title was, appropriately enough, *The Betrayal of Images*.[31] Cocteau predicted a whole new mixed genre, heralded by his own *The Wedding on the Eiffel Tower*, "in the margin" between theater, ballet, and light opera. This "revolution which flings doors wide open . . . ," he continued, would allow the "new generation" to "continue its experiments in which the fantastic, the dance, acrobatics, mime, drama, satire, music, and the spoken word combine. . . ."[32] *The Wedding on the Eiffel Tower*, moreover, includes a version of the classic chorus and the music-hall master of ceremonies, so that inconsistent styles and periods are jumbled together too.

A notable instance of the blending of media—as well as of the literary nature of the movement—is the invasion of surrealist art works in all media by literature in the form of titles for paintings, sculpture, plays, and (Satie's) musical compositions. These titles were often long, or oblique, or outright nonsensical: *Why Not Sneeze?* for example, is the title for a cageful of marble ice cubes plus thermometer by Duchamp; and *Three Pear-shaped Pieces* and *Dried-out Embryos* for musical pieces by Satie; and *Please* (*S'il vous plaît*) for a play by Breton and Soupault. Rather than elucidating or describing the art work, these titles often combine with it, extend it, to produce an unexpected effect—or, indeed, to produce the finished work. Titles often made puns on the art

31. *Le Trahison des Images*, or *L'air et la chanson* (1928–1929).
32. Cocteau, Préface to *The Wedding on the Eiffel Tower* in *Théâtre*, p. 47.

work, like dreams, or they added a threat: Max Ernst's *Two Children Menaced by a Nightingale*, for example, or Yves Tanguy's *Mama, Papa Is Wounded*. These titles were not meant to transmit information; they were meant, said Duchamp, apropos of his *In Advance of a Broken Arm* (showing a snow shovel), to "create another form, as if using another color." Often, as in the case of the *Nightingale* (and like the above-mentioned "pipe"), the caption was written prominently right across the canvas so as to make words literally part of the painting. Magritte's paintings were often named for famous books, such as Poe's *The Domaine of Arnheim*, Rousseau's *Rêveries du promeneur solitaire*, and Sade's *La philosophie dans le boudoir*.

Conversely, the nonliterary imagery of surrealism tended to draw its strength from implied verbal formulations—again an instance of the blending of media. Literature was translated into visual form, as occurred when Dali actually built a "rainy taxi" (a popular surrealist verbal construction) for an exhibition in 1938. Magritte has been called a "painter of epigrams."[33] In Apollinaire's play *The Breasts of Tiresias*, verbal puns slip from one medium to another. The play takes place in Zanzibar, for example, and the script calls for dice as a motif in the decor: *zanzibar* or *zanzi* is not only a place but also a dice game. Also, placards announce that, unlike the Seine, "notre scène" (our scene) is not at Paris (French pronunciation, which makes *Paris* sound like *pari*, or bet). Meanwhile two characters have just made a bet about where they are.

Since no traditional distinctions could be made in quality or kind, surrealist artists used materials not normally considered suitable for art, often in combination with conventional paints. Surrealism made happy use of the debris and waste products of society, the proliferating unlovely banal objects and mechanical

33. David Sylvester, *René Magritte*, p. 10.

relationships which were very often direct evidences of technology. Collages used ticket stubs, bottle labels, scraps of cloth and glass. Collages in an extra dimension, like sculptures, were called constructions. *Why Not Sneeze?* is an example. In 1936 Merle Oppenheim covered a cup, saucer, and spoon with fur and entitled the whole, appropriately enough, *Fur-Covered Cup, Saucer, and Spoon.* Constructions with moving parts and even live parts (tethered insects) appeared. Writers borrowed from life great masses of clichés and threw them whole into poems or plays. "Real" people such as Napoleon, Cleopatra, Mussolini, and Lloyd George appear as characters in otherwise totally fictional plays. Picasso's later play *Desire Caught by the Tail* has as characters Big Foot and Hunger. Noise music mixed with more conventional music in Satie's score for the ballet *Parade.* Kurt Schwitters put together inside his house constructions of wood and whatever else came to hand; he was building his environment, which he called *Merzbau* after some syllables which had once appeared by accident on a collage. (Eventually it took up the entire house, and he and his wife were forced to move out.) This is an example of mixing of materials and also of the refusal to distinguish between art to look at and art as an environment to live in.

Mixing of tone in all media is another evidence of the dissolution of all accepted categories in surrealist art. A play might include, for example, rhetorical philosophizing, nonsense doggerel, and conversational banalities, as does Rogert Vitrac's *The Mysteries of Love.* It might combine tragic romance and grotesque humor, as does Robert Desnos' *La Place de L'Étoile.*

Collages of all sorts also expressed another, related, concept which haunts critics in the arts today. If the universe is incoherent, composed of disparate phenomena of no intrinsic value, then all phenomena are equally valuable. Value judgments are impossible, at least in relation to art. It is impossible to weigh the quality of an object, or collection of objects, which claim to be

Cocteau uses an actress as a statue and a horse as a construction, and films them both. *Blood of a Poet.* Collection, the Museum of Modern Art, New York, Film Archive.

Dali devastates western culture by expanding a statue through other materials and dimensions. *The Venus de Milo of the Drawers* (1936). Courtesy of the Galerie du Dragon, Paris.

nothing but an arbitrarily chosen artifact of someone's life. And furthermore, since every phenomenon can play its indispensable role as a key to surreality, every phenomenon is equally valuable. Here surrealist philosophy seems to be confirming the popular spirit of the times: the undiscriminating delight in accumulation of mass-produced things, the breakdown of social classes, and possibly the reaction to an increasingly stratified and complex society.

In the theater, mixing of media is a traditional tendency as integral as the mixing of the art and the social situation in the theater event. Now electricity and film were added to gas lights, music, decor, language, and so on. In 1919, Yvan Goll startled the audience at his play *Mathusalem* by the introduction of film together with live stage action. (Wagner's vision of a *Gesamtkunstwerk* was already abroad, of course, and Gordon Craig, Appia, and Jessner were experimenting with technological ways of expanding stage possibilities.) The theater event, an intensified soirée, became a surrealist collage on the biggest possible scale: words, actions, situations, characters who are animate people, characters who are inanimate ideas or objects, music and dance and decor—plus the interaction of performers and audience.

Schwitters planned a *"Merz* total work of art"* in connection with his sketches for his *Merz* stage, mentioned above. His instructions for this total theater are worth quoting in some detail, for they present the general surrealist attitude with particular gusto.

. . . Up until now, a distinction was made between stage-set, text, and score in theatrical performances. Each factor was separately enjoyed. The Merz stage knows only the fusing of all factors into a composite work. Materials for the stage-set are all solid, liquid, and gaseous bodies, such as white wall, man, barbed wire entanglement, blue distance. . . . Take gigantic surfaces, conceived as infinite, cloak them in color and shift them menacingly. . . . Paste smoothing surfaces over one another . . . Make lines fight together and caress one another in generous tenderness. . . . Bend the lines, crack and smash angles . . . let a line rush by, tangible in wire. . . . Then take wheels and axles, hurl them up and make them sing (Mighty erections of aquatic giants). Axles dance mid-wheel roll globes barrels. Cogs flair teeth, find a sewing machine that yawns. . . . Take a dentist's drill, a meat grinder, a car-track scraper, take buses and pleasure cars, bicycles, tandems, and their tires, also ersatz wartime tires and deform them. Take lights and deform them as brutally as you can. Make locomotives crash into one another, curtains and portieres make threads of spider webs dance with window frames and break whimpering glass. Explode steam boilers to make railroad mist. Take petticoats and other kindred articles, shoes and false hair, also ice skates and throw them into place where they belong, and always at the right time. For all I care, take man-traps, automatic pistols, infernal machines, the tinfish and the funnel, all of course in an artistically deformed condition. Inner tubes are highly recommended. Take in short everything from the hairnet of the high class lady to the propeller of the S. S. Leviathan, always bearing in mind the dimensions required by the work.

Even people can be used. . . .

Now begin to wed your materials to one another. For example, you marry the oilcloth table cover to the Home Owners' Loan Association, you bring the lamp cleaner into a relationship with the marriage between Anna Blume and A-natural, concert pitch. . . . You make a human walk on his (her) hands and wear a hat on his (her) feet. . . . A splashing of foam.

And now begins the fire of musical saturation. Organs backstage sing and say: "Futt, futt." The sewing machine rattles along in the lead. A man in the wings says: "Bah." Another suddenly enters and says: "I am stupid." (All rights reserved.) Between them a clergyman kneels upside down and cries out and prays in a loud voice: "Oh mercy seethe and swarm disintegration of amazement Hallelujah boy, boy marry drop of water." A water pipe drips uninhibited monotony. Eight.[34]

In the light of the breakdown of genre distinctions, it is not surprising that most surrealist artists worked in more than one

34. William S. Rubin, *Dada Surrealism*, p. 57.

medium, refusing to classify themselves rigidly as painter or poet. The poet Francis Picabia drew. Artaud, as we saw, directed and designed costumes. Cocteau, who was only on the fringes of the movement, dabbled in all the arts. And all of them took part freely in performances and readings of each others' works; Duchamp, for example, appeared nude in the character of Adam in the ballet *Relâche*. Especially, confirming the essentially literary impulse of the movement, whatever their primary medium, almost all the surrealists wrote. Duchamp wrote poetry and prose. Henri Rousseau (not an actual member of the movement) wrote two delightful plays: a comedy entitled *A Visit to the Exposition of 1889* and an old-fashioned melodrama, performed recently for the first time, entitled *The Vengeance of a Russian Orphan Girl*.

In token of the breakdown of logical categories, individual surrealist art works generally had the quality called objectivation: they were composed of specific, clearly identifiable parts. Only in the manipulation of these parts was a possible abstraction, symbolic reference, or aesthetic value invoked. Similarly, Pronko speaks of more recent avant-garde playwrights' use of "concrete visual images to suggest a metaphysical bias" and suggests as examples the hats and tree in Beckett's *Waiting for Godot* and the doors in Ionesco's *The Chairs*. Furthermore, only in the juxtaposition or dislocation of these parts could surprising glimpses of surreality be attained. These fragments retained their individual concrete identities. They could be combined but not synthesized. It is the connection between the parts that operates; as in cinema it is the connection between the shots.

This chaos of fragments resisted unification; unity seemed to the surrealists too artificially rational a concept in the face of a chaotic universe. The unity of surrealist art works, like the definition of one object or another as surrealist art, is a matter of the artist's sole and arbitrary decision. Artaud observed that in film, it is the camera that imposes instantaneous temporary unity on whatever it frames, however arbitrary or uncontrolled the contents of the frame.[35] Of course there is also unity insofar as the whole work came from one artist's subconscious. Apollinaire's concept of the internal frame in cubist paintings was, in effect, whatever element of the painting informed the rest—and was, besides, most characteristic of the individual painter.[36] Closer to this concept is Tzara's description of ideal Dada poetry: ". . . a rhythm which one neither sees nor hears; beam from an interior arrangement toward a constellation of order."[37] Again reference to the theater is illuminating, for this ideal rhythm seems like the "tragic rhythm" which Francis Fergusson analyzes as the heart and structure of classical tragedies.[38]

One has the feeling, however, of a surrealist impulse to extract something positive, even definite, from chaos, and perhaps from the inescapable modern doubt over what constitutes a genuine perception. Nonrational and largely nonsensory and nonemotional, surrealist art operated through ideas, or perhaps through the single huge idea of idealessness. This seems connected with the literary or verbal quality which we noted earlier. Although the surrealists shunned abstractions, which are intellectual constructs, there is an abstract, cerebral quality to much of their art, even when the mood is angry or gay: a still place inside the chaos. As a critic said of Magritte's painted images: they have "intense affective import . . . with great immediacy but no sensuous correlative, just as in dreams the action is all in one's head."[39] Perhaps this quality arises from the thrust of their artistic techniques,

35. ". . . dans la mesure où le cinéma est laissé seul en face des objets il leur impose un ordre"—Artaud, "La vieillesse précoce du cinéma" in *Oeuvres Complètes* III, p. 96.

36. Apollinaire, *Les peintres cubistes* (Paris: Eugène Figuiere et Cie, 1913), p. 36.

37. ". . . un rythme qu'on ne voit et qu'on n'entend pas; rayon d'un groupement intérieur vers une constellation d'ordre"—Tzara, "Note sur la poésie," in *Lampisteries*, p. 106.

38. Francis Fergusson, *The Idea of a Theater.*

39. Sylvester, *Magritte*, p. 1.

Marcel Duchamp, *To be Looked At (From the Other Side of the Glass) With One Eye, Close to, For Almost an Hour* (1918). Framed double glass panel with oil paint, collage, lens, etc. This construction puts together many materials, including words. It also includes the spectator's participation. Furthermore, like Duchamp's similar *Large Glass,* it evidently includes cracks from moving between exhibitions.

A mechanical dislocation of vision transforms this matter-of-fact image from René Clair's film *Entr'acte*. Permission, Cinémathèque Française, Paris.

which move from principle toward experience. Perhaps it is their refusal to use symbolic images, which make coherent connections on several levels simultaneously, that makes their art seem narrowed despite a commitment to chaos. Certainly this cerebral quality is related to the French classicism within which most of the surrealists were trained, no matter how hard they rebelled. It may be simply that the surrealists tried to exist at extremes whereas most people are used to a kind of ordinary middling human level of existence, and that this gives their art its rather cool, sometimes metallic, still, and almost ascetic quality. It offers experience purified of emotions and flesh.

The drive toward instantaneity which is revealed by every aspect of surrealist art is part of the same attempt to crystallize chaos. The surrealists seem to yearn to intensify existence rather than diffuse it: to gather up Bergson's duration-in-time into the present instant. A conspicuous evidence of this drive is that the majority of surrealist art works do not exist in ongoing time. They are paintings, constructions, or short poems. Presumably their creation was instantaneous; certainly their absorption, as we shall see, was to be instantaneous. Novels, which build in time and even use time as an element of content, were alien to surrealism. The surrealist urge toward theater which we have noted seems contradictory here, since plays inevitably progress in time. But, as one means of resolving the contradiction, surrealist plays (and musical compositions) were characteristically extremely short. Surrealist playwrights and Satie combated the cumulative nature of their media in several ways. They repeated words, sounds, musical or verbal phrases, so as to stay in the same place, as it were, and finally to negate any sense of ongoing time within the work; plays whose chronology can never be established do the same. They avoided developing themes of any sort; in any case, such development would have constituted a structure. It is also true, of course, that it is difficult to sustain an art work which

refuses to develop—unless as a sort of collage of movements—
and this circumstance may be a further factor in the marked brevity of most surrealist musical compositions and plays. We may
speculate, in any case, that the tension between surrealism's will
to negate time and the art form's will to progress in time is one
more source of energy for surrealist drama.

We have already mentioned film's property of arresting time
in connection with the film maker's absolute control. Although
films do progress in time, the entire duration of the action can be
compressed into a physical reel of film. They seem to synthesize,
as it were vertically, all stimuli into an instant of effect. Also the
film maker can use the medium to make time seem to go back-
wards or to stop entirely. Artaud wrote an unproduced scenario
called *18 Seconds* whose whole purpose lies in this playing with
time. We watch the hero watching eighteen seconds pass on a
clock; meanwhile the film lasts an hour or two. In principle, the
time difference consists of his fantasies; but this is never spelled
out, and the focus of the film, as evidenced by its title, lies precisely in the relativity of time. Unlike surrealist plays, which
tended to be brief so as not to dissipate their force and to exist
only for a supreme instant, film made it possible to sustain the
instant. Susan Sontag described film in words which we could
use about surrealist theater and really about all the surrealist arts:
"a compact theater-experience which approaches . . . the condition of painting";[40] and in this connection we might remember
that many of the early film makers were painters.

Like the Eiffel Tower, surrealist art came from the disintegration of old aesthetics in the face of a fresh redefinition of art.
Happy to be conspicuous, it advertised its own philosophical
bases and its differences from everything that surrounded it. It

40. Susan Sontag in *Tulane Drama Review*, Vol. II, No. 1, p. 36.

also reveals, on analysis, attitudes which all Paris did in fact come to share.

All the aspects of surrealist art described in this chapter amount to evidences of the surrealist artist's effort to condense all possible experience into a single cosmic experience. Our next chapter will deal with the surrealist artist's counterpart, his audience: his second self, who shares, expands, and fulfills the surrealist art experience.

CHAPTER FIVE

The Surrealist Audience

The surrealist art experience was incomplete in theory and practice without the participation of an audience. Surrealist art was, as Marcel Duchamp described the "image" in his own paintings and sculptures, "an act which must be completed by the spectator."[1] According to surrealist philosophy, the instant of intense reconciliation through an art work in which such completion occurred was the opportunity for mutual contact with the universal essence which both artist and spectator both contained and reflected. "It is the spectator who, through a kind of inner 'osmosis,' deciphers and interprets the work's inner qualification, relates them to the external world, and thus completes the creative cycle."[2] What art is to do, in other words, still quoting Duchamp, is to "break down the association between the object and onlooker and in breaking down these limitations free the spirit of man."[3]

In a limited sense, we who look at the spectacle of the Surrealist movement are its audience, and this chapter is about our experiences: the effect on us of the phenomena contained in the preceding chapters. But before we can look at the surrealist techniques for enforcing reconciliation of audience and artist and surreality, we must recall how integrally the audience was part of

1. Dreier and Echaurren, *Duchamp's Glass*, n.p.
2. Tomkins, *Bride and Bachelors*, p. 9. He is quoting from a lecture given by Duchamp in 1957.
3. Dreier and Echaurren, *Duchamp's Glass*, n.p.

all surrealist art activity. The surrealists were a community; all together they expressed a common perception. Surrealists considered that the word of any one of their fellows spoke for-all. This was especially true since they were all friends as well as colleagues. A spectator who was an initiate was thus already almost literally at one with the artist. And this was true even of a bourgeois outsider, if he was so affected by a specific art experience as to be lifted beyond his limitations and into touch with surreality—that is, it was true during the instant of his response.

This basic oneness of artist and audience is visible in several aspects of surrealist art. We have seen how at café soirées, for example, artist and audience sat together and easily exchanged roles. We have also seen how Tzara's Dada play *The Gas Heart* incorporated this pattern by including politely uncomplimentary comments on the play, delivered by an actor who stood in the audience area facing the stage acting out, as it were, the disintegration of the distinction between artist and audience. The action of Vitrac's play *The Mysteries of Love* actually begins not onstage but in a stage box with the houselights on.

Similarly we have also noted the surrealist attention to environments as an art form capable of enclosing artist and spectator equally and simultaneously. Kurt Schwitters built his Merzbau all around him. He also envisioned, as we saw, a "radical and hallucinatory Merz experience, one that would have turned an Environment into a Happening,"[4] to take place in an area constructed as follows: "Take gigantic surfaces, conceived as infinite, cloak them in color and shift them menacingly. . . ."[5] Hans Arp and others decorated a Strasbourg restaurant with wildly geometric murals. Max Ernst covered the interior of Éluard's house at Eaubonne with paintings: ceilings, doors, and all. The house

4. Rubin, *Dada, Surrealism*, p. 57.
5. Ibid.

was transformed into a "jewel box of dreams" of which one guest remembers most vividly the "unprecedented flush" of a giant strawberry painted on the bathroom wall.[6]

The environment of surrealist exhibitions was as important as the art works on the walls. For the 1938 exhibition at the Galerie Beaux Arts in Paris,, Marcel Duchamp "designed a great central hall with a pool surrounded by real grass."[7] The decor also included twelve hundred coalsacks hanging from the ceiling, a carpet of dead leaves, and four large beds. "At the opening of the exhibition the odor of roasting coffee filled the hall. A recording of a German army marching song was broadcast, and a girl performed a dance around the pool."[8] Flashlights were loaned to the visitors for illuminating the paintings.

Beyond the basic unity of all members and sympathizers of the Surrealist movement, however, we see that the thrust of every surrealist art work is toward forcing artist and audience into instantaneous temporary personal union. And for this union to occur, the artist himself had to be in position to participate. Recognition that reconciliation between artist and spectator is at the heart of the surrealist art experience puts in a new light the surrealist concept of the artist: his need to encompass personally the entire creative experience, and his drive to be creator rather than imitator.

In order to share the intense moment of reconciliation with the spectator, the surrealist artist felt he had to keep contact between himself and the audience as direct as possible. We can see his struggle to do so particularly clearly in the case of the dramatist-director. For in the theater, paradoxically, although the audience is materially present at the moment of performance, the drama-

6. Patrick Waldberg, "Max Ernst chez Paul Éluard" in *Max Ernst peintures pour Paul Éluard*, p. 13.
7. Rubin, *Dada, Surrealism*, p. 154.
8. Ibid. See photo, p. 87.

tist's contact with them is threatened because he is only one of several participants and may not even be present.

One way to establish a single theater artist to balance the audience and share reconciliation with them—and thereby make the theater event genuinely surrealist—is to create a "universal athlete" or a collective approximation of one. Or, the dramatist or director alone might take over so many separate functions as to become himself almost a "universal athlete." Or he might take over the entire act of creation by reducing the actors to extensions of himself. This he might accomplish by literally writing for marionettes; we have seen that marionettes were popular in surrealist and contemporary thinking about theater. Or he can prevent live actors from intercepting the current which is to run between himself and the audience by making them into live marionettes, mere mouthpieces for his words. Forced to employ several human bodies with voices, he may resist yielding up any part of the creative process to them and may undercut their ability to transcend their individual personalities and create independently. For instance, he may sabotage the actors' traditional function by allowing for no individual characterization in the text; he may name them "The Young Man" or "The Equestrian" or "The Man in Evening Dress." He may have them pantomime actions, to be narrated by someone else, as in *The Wedding on the Eiffel Tower*. Also, if characters never speak or behave in such a way as to allow for characterization or illusion of life, the audience will respond only to the dramatist's words rather than to the actors' impersonations. Also, the dramatist may choose an acting style to render his actors personally nonhuman: mechanical vehicles for his creation. He may direct them to declaim in Ubuesque style, formal and eccentric. He may, like Apollinaire, have them speak sporadically through megaphones. He may contrive costumes and masks which submerge their opportunities for acting in any conventional sense.

At the same time, the repudiation of mimesis in the theater, as in other arts, indirectly furthered reconciliation of dramatist with audience. The elimination of the illusion of real-life events onstage prevented the spectator from "feeling for" the fictional characters who seemed to be suffering up there. Furthermore, lack of action in the conventional mimetic sense onstage may be said to force the audience to supply an action by the energy of their response.

The insistence on direct personal contact between dramatist and spectator gives us yet another insight into the surrealist affinity with cinema. We have already noted that the cinema is controlled by a single artist who creates his own universe. Now that statement can be corroborated by Artaud's observation that in the cinema "the actor is only a living sign. . . . Chaplin plays Chaplin, Pickford plays Pickford, Fairbanks plays Fairbanks. They are the film. . . . That's why they don't exist. Thus nothing comes between the work and us. . . ."[9] With film emerged the nonmimetic form of acting which, as we have seen, has been called nonmatrixed: free of the matrices of time-place-character.[10] Rather, the actor puts his identity at the service of the dramatist, as does most notably the movie star, whom we talk about in terms of personality and qualities rather than in terms of the roles he plays or even his talent for acting. A half-century after Artaud, Richard Gilman commented on the way film "gets around" the "tradition of impersonation" through "its very abstraction, its mythic reality."[11] So even at a distance, the film maker is in a sense alone with his audience.

Artaud, our ultimate surrealist and pioneer film maker, was always passionately concerned with drama's effect upon the audi-

9. "Au cinéma l'acteur n'est qu'un signe vivant . . . Charlot joue Charlot, Pickford joue Pickford, Fairbanks joue Fairbanks. Ils sont le film. C'est pourquoi ils n'existent pas. Rien donc s'interpose entre l'oeuvre et nous. . . ."— Artaud, *Oeuvres Complètes*, Vol. III, p. 74.

10. Kirby, *Happenings*, p. 17. See above, p. 59.

11. Richard Gilman, *The New Republic* (Nov. 9, 1968).

ence. He consistently spoke of drama in terms of this effect, and defined his Theater of Cruelty in terms of it, as opposed to dramatic form or story material. In a particularly famous passage in *The Theater and Its Double*, Artaud described the operation of the ideal theater upon the community of spectators as a plague, so strong and visceral is its action to be.[12] He also spoke of it in terms of the lancing of an abcess, echoing the traditional notion of catharsis along with the surrealist notion of intense contact.[13] Later, retaining the powerful persistent physicality of these images but shifting their focus as he concentrated increasingly on films, he compared the effect of film upon the audience to the operation of a poison which "works directly upon the grey matter of the brain."[14]

Certainly film's ability to force the audience to project themselves onto the screen, to "penetrate the screen"[15] and thus enter the creation, is relevant to Apollinaire's prophesy that a new cinematographic sensibility "was one of surrealism's most important goals."[16] It may also explain the astonishing number of surrealists who experimented with film between 1918 and 1925: André Breton, Marcel Duchamp, Man Ray, Salvador Dali, Yvan Goll, Philippe Soupault, Robert Desnos, Louis Aragon, Francis Picabia. Breton, who spent entire army leaves with Jacques Vaché stumbling from one movie theater right into another, said that it was in the movie theater "that is celebrated the only absolutely modern mystery,"[17] and of course "mystery" in that religious sense signi-

12. Antonin Artaud, *The Theater and Its Double*, translated by Mary Caroline Richards (New York: Grove Press, 1958), p. 25.
13. Ibid., p. 31.
14. "Le cinéma est un excitant remarquable. Il agit sur la matière grise du cerveau directement"; and also, "Le cinéma a surtout la vertu d'un poison"—Artaud, "Réponse à une enquête," *Oeuvres Complètes*, III, p. 74.
15. Kyrou, *Surréalisme au Cinéma*, p. 178. M. Kyrou uses this phrase in discussing Marcel Duchamp's experiments in film.
16. "Une nouvelle sensibilité cinématographique est en train de naître . . . elle est un des buts les plus importants du surréalisme."—Apollinaire, Il Y A in *Oeuvres Poétiques*, p. 253.
17. Breton in Kyrou, *Surréalisme au Cinéma*, p. 22. See above.

fies that the congregation of spectators is participating in the priest's act.

Reconciliation of artist and audience must be complete for the surrealists to consider the art work complete. To this end the audience had to be fully open to the experience of surreality— had to be prepared to spontaneously "project themselves" into it. Surrealist techniques for inducing free response to art works were very similar to techniques which induced free creativity. They aimed to get past the barrier of ingrained habits of rationality to free the spectator's inner self, the essence of self which was both intensely personal and universal.

In film, and other media too, one way in which the surrealists tried to evoke full and spontaneous response was to draw the audience into the work by means of a kind of hypnosis. Dreams and subconscious material, hallucinatory images, disorientation of perspective in painting, verbal repetition which may even be prolonged and seem boring—all these drew the audience deeply into the work. Prolonged repetition of sounds or words has the primitive power of drumbeats or ritual incantation. Such repetition ultimately passed monotony to become intolerable pressure on the spectator. Dramaturgically, as in Vitrac's dream play *Free Entry*, the artist might arrange for a surrogate dreamer to guide the spectator into the experience and order the scenes accordingly in a whirlpool of concentric layers of reality. In all cases, by cutting the spectator's connections with the outside world he knows, the surrealist artist forced him to inhabit the world of the art work, totally and intensely.

But the primary way in which the surrealists tried to force the audience into reconciliation through the art work was through attack. Attack is basic to Dada and the Surrealist movement, and for several reasons. First of all, it was fun. The private and public behavior of Dada and the surrealists was calculated in terms of constant attacks, especially against the bourgeoisie. They adored

Jarry's protagonist King Ubu for the ringing "merdre" by which
he had introduced himself to the gasping world. Tzara said that
"every act is a cerebral gunshot."[18]

Acts of provocation through art events had social and political
implications too. For Dada especially, the audience was a member of society, and therefore committed to the bourgeois establishment, and therefore the enemy. So attacking him, especially
obscenely, was a virtuous act. Boxer Arthur Cravan's deliberately
undressing himself onstage while belching loudly, Philippe Soupault's yelling insults from the stage into the house, Jacques
Rigaud's counting aloud the automobiles and the pearls of the
lady visitors as they entered a show of Max Ernst's collages—
these were notable examples of the attitude. Similarly, at the first
performance of *The Gas Heart* by Tristan Tzara, many in the
audience soon walked out indignantly; working-class people who
lived in the neighborhood of the theater, they had been promised
a lecture on money management. This sort of deception was a
favorite Dada prank. Once they advertised falsely that Charlie
Chaplin would appear at a soirée. Naturally they drew great
crowds, and were gratified to watch the people grow first im-
patient, then disappointed, and finally furious. The theater seems
to be particularly suitable for this stance of attack, since it demands the presence of attacker and victim.

Sometimes the attack which Dada and the surrealists promoted
was actually physical. Another performance of *The Gas Heart* in
1923 was interrupted before the first-act curtain by a brawl so
fierce that the actors eventually stopped contributing their part
to the general commotion, so that the performance—or at least,
the script—was never finished. It was on this occasion, before
the police arrived, that Breton broke de Massot's arm with his

18. "Tout acte est un coup de revolver cérébral."—Tzara, "M. Aa nous en-
voie ce Manifeste" (1920) in *Lampisteries*, p. 49.

elegant cane. (This brawl is considered by some to mark the definitive organizational split of the Surrealist movement from Dada.) Tzara was rumored to have deliberately instigated this brawl by the use of a claque; the same had been reported of Jarry at the opening of *Ubu Roi* in 1898. At the first showing of the Buñuel and Dali film *Un Chien Andalou*, people threw hats and sticks at the screen.

But surrealism converted the Dada attack into a larger and more positive aesthetic action. For surrealism, attack was not only a pleasure and a social duty, but also a necessary means to philosophical reconciliation through art. The audience must be prevented from responding to an art rationally or with the conventional emotional empathy that regularly answers a recognizable social experience. (Thus no plays, as plays have been traditionally defined in the West since Greek tragedy, were acceptable surrealist experiences.) It must not be fed an art work whose form or content is in any way comfortably familiar to it; such art works were the products and perpetuators of a stultified bourgeois society. (The rejection of art forms on grounds that they are bourgeois was in any case not new in France. "Bourgeois" was a war cry for the young romantics who brawled in defense of Victor Hugo's *Hernani* in 1832.) Rather, the audience must respond freely to the art work. He must respond instantly, without stopping to think. (Again we think of the theater, the art form in which the spectator is propelled into an ongoing experience.) Only then can he truly participate in a union with the artist and with the essence of life. But since the spectator—even a sympathetic one—is unlikely to be capable of such openness on his own, the artist must get past the guard which protects but also imprisons him and reach his soul. This the artist does by first surprising and shocking him and only later, when his guard is down, going further.

Several forms of this campaign of attack on rational response

Portrait of an Imbecile. Philippe Soupault exhibited this framed mirror at a show of surrealist art. The startling title, creation of an event, integration of the spectator into the art work, bold definition of what constitutes the art work, and general prankishness are all typically surrealist. Photo permission Roger Viollet, Paris.

Mlle. Hélène Vanel performed in this surrealist environment as part of the Surrealist Exhibition in Paris in 1938. The title of her dance has been recorded variously as "Danse macabre" and "The Unconsummated Act." Permission, Keystone Press Agency, New York and Paris. See p. 80.

are inherent in surrealist art works. For example, when Marcel Duchamp exhibited his "Fountain," he knew it was an attack on his spectators—that they would feel attacked, at any rate. For them a urinal was just not art. In the same spirit Tzara impudently subtitled a play "the biggest hoax of the century," knowing that the play uses the paraphernalia of serious drama and poetry only to tease and exasperate by their lack of substance.

But if systems of values, including aesthetic ones, have all been arbitrarily imposed on an inchoate relativistic universe, then sensibilities trained by one system or another need not be coddled. On the contrary, the fresh reorganization of phenomena for the spectator, who is chained to old perceptions, is a primary function of art and the sudden shift is quite salutary. Mallarmé had redefined his perceptions drastically in speaking of margins "like silence" which were as much part of the poem as were the words.[19] John Cage was to make the same leap in defining silences as *part* of his music.[20]

Similarly, a popular verbal mechanism to attack and disorient the spectator is the cliché in poems and plays, which is used as part of an effort to free the words from the meanings. Clichés swim to the surface in the midst of serious language—or nonsense—and then sink, the way snatches of the Marseillaise tease Satie's hearers. Repeated clichés not only bring into relief the meaninglessness which has resulted from the words' excessive use in blank social intercourse; they also reach back to the words' essential meaninglessness by shaking them loose from their common meanings. Then, too, clichés are a social convention which the surrealists enjoyed mocking.

The sudden unexpected dislocation or juxtaposition of objects

19. ". . . blancs . . . comme silence" in Mallarmé's poem "Un Coup de dés jamais n'abolira le hasard," a poem which greatly impressed Apollinaire in his youth. *Oeuvres de Stéphane Mallarmé*, p. 455.

20. John Cage, *Silence: Lectures and Writings*. Also Tomkins, *The Bride and the Bachelors*, Chapter Two.

or images shocks the spectator into a realm beyond rationality. Adrift, his sense of fit distinctions temporarily disintegrates, and he can experience to the full such crazy combinations of extremes as the verbal image "rainy taxi," as a hanger nailed to the floor and called sculpture, as dancers moving not to music but to noise or to speech or to silence, as slapstick immediately following melodrama, as a jet of blood spurting from the wrist of a god.

Another kind of attack consists of forms of mystification. The play *Please* by Breton and Soupault, like most surrealist poetry, operates through endless vertiginous shifts in language, which onstage or in films can be translated into shifts of situations as well. *Please* first accomplishes by this means the repeated demolition of expectations formed by the audience's experience of life or of conventional drama. Action and dialogue suggest ideas, then contradict or undercut them. They mystify the spectator without providing a clue—or else provide several mutually contradictory clues. They destroy even the illusion of causality, chronology, or logic. They make the spectator feel helpless to figure anything out, so that in the end he is the more receptive on the artist's terms. Habit forces the spectator's intellect to respond doggedly to all stimuli, verbal or visual. This allows the artist to trigger great explosions of associated ideas, then to short-circuit each one and proceed instantly to pile on the next. Out of these masses an experience should surface for the spectator. And if the original stimuli arose genuinely from the artist's own essence and were collected by his own spontaneous associations, the spectator is truly reconciled with the artist and beyond.

We see a particular verbal refinement of all these techniques in Tzara's (Dada) absolutely plotless *The Gas Heart*, which provokes by tantalizingly denying all possibility of making sense out of the words despite their normal conversational patterns. The syntax of the text of *The Gas Heart* is a mechanism of unexpected juxtapositions and disorientations. Combinations of

Two stages in the paroxysm of violence experienced by a character in Buñuel's film *L'Age D'or.* The action with feather pillows is rather ludicrous, reminiscent of a scene in *The Gold Rush*; the surrealists admired Chaplin. Collection, the Museum of Modern Art, New York, Film Archive.

clauses which begin with signals to orderly thought processes, such as "who" and "of which," camouflage groups of words which mean nothing at all. Apparently logical transitions do the same, as in the proposition: "The air came with blue eyes, *that's why* he takes aspirin all the time." (The italics are mine.) An audience conditioned to react rationally to language is shocked over and over again, while the bourgeois mind which created and clings to rationality is mocked. The unexpected juxtaposition of words within conventional patterns creates a momentary giddy sensation of serious conversation gone awry. Syntactical arrangement and rapid repetitions of words make patches of meaningful conversation seem to emerge. But these meanings dissolve again instantly. For example, bickerings seem to flare up, as when, after a number of variations on the phrase "Everyone knows you," Mouth enters and says, "Everyone does not know me." But words without any such link follow and the audience must again swallow mindlessness.

Similarly, dramatically rather than simply verbally, Tzara shocks by the very fact of a play which is not mimetic. There seems to be dramatic contact between two speakers, but the impression arises from the form of the speeches and not from what they say individually, or do, or who they are. Rhythms, vocabularly, the syntax of the speeches—all create a spurious tone of relationship between the speakers, as if they were carrying on a dialogue. So do the consistent and inexplicable names of the dramatis personae: Nose, Mouth, Ear, Neck, Eye.

The complaints of hostile outsiders at Dada and surrealist theater events from the beginning illustrate both a possible result of this mystification and a possible further reason for its use. The mass of stimuli can submerge the experience by exhausting the spectator's power to respond; he feels bored. However, Dada and surrealist poets and dramatists (and the composer Satie) tended overwhelmingly to limit their pieces in length, so that the effects did remain instantaneous. Also, devices of shock and surprise in action, as well as the frequent sharpness and felicity of verbal and visual imagery, were the artists' allies in blasting through to fresh responses from the spectators.

On one level, surrealist attack operates on the level of surprise and brings to surrealist art a kind of freshness and a mood of constant wonder. On another level, attack is deeper and darker and involves violence and humor, the twin moods of dreams.

The surrealists believed in violence and in violent repudiation of everything the bourgeoisie seemed to revere as culture. Their disputes with other factions, too, often erupted into fistfights or even duels. Jacques Vaché, who lived the paradigmatic surrealist life, preached the gratuitous act of violence (a term later associated with the French Existentialists) and wore a sword. The surrealists loved Punch and Judy shows, in which the puppets slam each other to puppet-death over and over again.

King Ubu, whom the surrealists adored, was in the habit of violently overturning all obstacles to his will. These included human obstacles (the king of Poland, whom he killed in *Ubu Roi*) or spiritual obstacles (his own conscience, whom he stuffed head first down a toilet in *Ubu cocu* or *Ubu Cuckolded*). The violence further extended to the audience, who were shocked, pleasantly or unpleasantly, by the "merdre" as by other forms of surrealist provocation.

In art, the surrealist violence shocked the spectator and filled him with dread, opening him to surrealist experiences. They evoked dreams which were usually nightmares, hinting at violence as yet untapped. They tried literally to do violence to the audience's perceptions. Their plays are full of blows and screams, as their soirées involved direct insults to the patrons. At the end of Apollinaire's *The Breasts of Tiresias*, Thérèse-Tirésias plays with her red and blue balloon-breasts, calling them, in a typically swooping surrealist metaphor, "birds of my frailty." They are

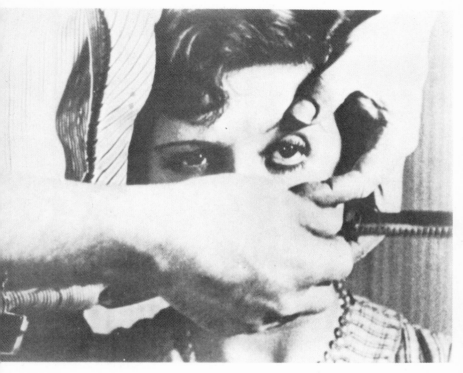

This action, performed very simply and matter-of-factly early in Buñuel's film *Un Chien Andalou,* always forces gasps and moans from the audience. It is directly preceded by a shot of the moon cut by a cloud. Collection, the Museum of Modern Art, New York, Film Archive.

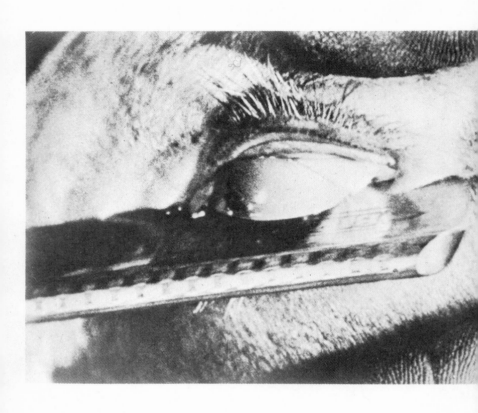

attached to her by strings and she makes them dance merrily. Then she produces a lighter and explodes them before the audience's eyes. This is a gesture of surreal violence, whether we see the explosion on the level of pretty balloons or on the level of breasts—or on the level of her very existence as a woman, since immediately thereafter she sprouts a moustache. In *The Wedding on the Eiffel Tower,* a child shoots the entire wedding party, his family, to get at some macaroons. Vitrac's *The Mysteries of Love* is especially full of incidents of fights, dismemberment, blood, like this one:

LEA: It's that he would open my belly, that one.

DOVIC: Noggin.

LEA: With his beard.

DOVIC: Oh, no! No scandal here, right? I protest, Lea. (*He slaps her.*) I always loved you. (*He pinches her.*) I still love you. (*He bites her.*) You must give me credit for that. (*He pulls her ears.*) Did I have cold sweats? (*He spits in her face.*) I caressed your breasts and your cheeks. (*He kicks her.*) All there was was yours. (*He makes as if to strangle her.*) You left. (*He shakes her violently.*) Did I hold it against you? (*He hits her several times with his fist.*) I am good. (*He throws her down on the ground.*) I have already forgiven you. (*He drags her around the stage box by her hair.*)

—and this one:

LEA: (*to the audience*)

        I love Patrice. Oh, I love his guts. Oh, I love that clown. Oh, I love that clown. From all sides, on all facings, in all forms, Look at them, Patrice. Listen to them. Oh, oh, oh!

        (*She laughs in peals.*)

A VOICE: (*in the audience*)

        But why? Just heavens! Why? Are you all sick?

LEA: Madly.

VOICE: Are you mad?

PATRICE: Madly.

ANOTHER   (*in the audience*)
VOICE: You hear them, Martine?
          (*a shot*)

ANOTHER   You hear them, Marie?
VOICE: (*a shot*)

ANOTHER   You hear them, Julie?
VOICE: (*a shot*)

ANOTHER   You hear them, Teresa?
VOICE: (*a shot*)

ANOTHER   You hear them, Esther?
VOICE: (*a shot*)

SEVERAL
VOICES: Kill me! Kill him! Kill her! Mercy! Pardon! The child!
          (*Tumult, cries, shots. Suddenly the house lights go out.
          Instant silence. . . .*)

At the end of the play Patrice shoots the Author and then Lea
fires into the audience, so that the very last line is Patrice's:
"What have you done, Lea? What have you done? You've just
killed a spectator."

In film, the kinds of images which a film maker can project
carry more potential violence even than stage action can. Artaud's scenario *The Butcher's Revolt* is full of menace and
slaughter. In *Un Chien Andalou,* Buñuel shows, among other
images whose fame attests to the power they retain over viewers,
a razor slicing slowly through an eyeball and ants eating their
way out of the palm of a hand. Again, the cerebral quality of the
violence is striking: a kind of abstract shock.

Laughter as the "violent reaction to something unknown"[21]

---

21. Duchamp, quoted in Dreier and Echaurreu, *Duchamp's Glass,* n.p.

René Magritte, *Le Viol* (1934). Oil. Collection of George Melly, London.

The same sort of joking attack as *Le Viol,* but more amusing than shocking. Max Ernst, *Oiseau-Tête* (variously exhibited as *Ladybird, Woman Bird)* (1934). Cast bronze. Collection of Mr. John W. Barnum, Washington, D.C.

was one of the responses the surrealists encouraged. They were very interested in the nature of the comic. In 1917 Vaché wrote that humor is "a sense of . . . the theatrical (and joyless) uselessness of everything, when one knows."[22] But for most surrealists, somewhat later, when the movement had formulated its principles more firmly, humor had a more positive role to play.

Breton proclaimed that "the laugh has taken on a metaphysical dimension"[23] starting with Jarry's *Ubu Roi*. Coining the expression "black humor," Breton described surrealist humor as a "higher revolt of the mind." Jarry's humor had "unbalanced life at its center of gravity."[24] The surrealists' laughter expressed their perception of the mad progressive unbalance of the world around them, as well as, perhaps, their sense of the comparative ineffectuality of the purely personal positive moments to be salvaged from the tornado. It has also the combination of mirth and hysteria which is characteristic of their youth.

Comedy was often a form of surrealist attack on bourgeois tradition. Magritte's later parody of David's famous portrait of Madame Récamier, reclining on her chaise longue, is an example.[25] So is the surrealist fondness for clichés, which indeed go further and mock all language. Apollinaire's *The Breasts of Tiresias* includes obvious literary parodies, especially of classical tragic tirades. *Cloud Handkerchief* is full of references to *Hamlet*, apparently parodic in intent. *Un Chien Andalou* makes fun of contemporary silent film conventions by inserting, for no reason, such standard captions as "Eight Years Later," "Sixteen Years Earlier," and "In the Spring," and by stipulating a florid tango to accompany a pursuit. Early in *The Wedding on the Eiffel*

22. ". . . un sens de . . . l'inutilité théâtrale (et sans joie) de tout, quand on sait."—Vaché, *Lettres*, p. 9.
23. ". . . le rire a pris une dimension métaphysique."—Clancier, *Rimbaud*, p. 151.
24. Breton, *Anthologie de l'humeur noire*, p. 5.
25. Béhar, *Roger Vitrac*, p. 155.

Tower, a telegram falls from the sky, causing the narrator to announce gravely that "the plot thickens." Later a character says, in what the surrealists considered typical bourgeois fashion: "Since these mysteries are beyond me, let's pretend we're organizing them."

Furthermore, "in surrealist hands humor becomes a weapon, deriding the importance of reality."[26] Comic grotesqueries disarmed the spectator, put him off guard so he could perceive that contrast between the real and the imagined which Bergson said lay at the core of the absurd.[27] In *Un Chien Andalou* the young man suddenly has hair instead of a mouth; the young woman sees this, gasps, and quickly inspects her armpit, which has become hairless. In Vitrac's play *Victor* a nine-year-old boy is full-grown and wise enough to unnerve his parents; in his play *Médor* a talking dog has a secret life as popular suave man(dog)-about-town.

Puns expose the impotence of language to make reality rational; they are jokes at the expense of language. Puns hint at mysteriously coinciding layers of meaning, and it is only to be expected that the surrealists reveled in them. Marcel Duchamp named a book *Marchand du sel* (read it aloud) and carried on elaborately punning correspondence with friends. He playfully copied the Mona Lisa, gave her a beard and moustache, and entitled the whole *LHOOQ* (the title slightly obscene when read aloud: *Elle a chaud au cul* or *She has hot pants.*) His *Tu m'* (again, the title a hint of obscenity in itself, but this time altogether separate from the work) shows a painted rip in material which is actually held together by real safety pins. Magritte's paintings of paintings standing on easels in front of

26. Matthews, *Introduction* . . . , p. 115.
27. ". . . comic illusion is similar to dream illusion . . . the logic of the comic is the logic of dreams."—Bergson, "Laughter" in *Comedy,* p. 181, also p. 87.

windows confuse painting with window; his paintings of mirrors reflecting the wrong side of a man are part of the same mode. Trompe l'oeil, which the surrealists did not discover but adopted enthusiastically, is a sort of visual pun. Surrealist play dialogue is rich in puns, some referring complexly to the action onstage. Picabia and Satie named their ballet *Relâche*, which on a theater poster means "No Show Tonight": thus it was almost impossible to advertise a performance or to enquire about it at the box office without causing confusion, and with a straight face. The Surrealist movement celebrated nonrationality. The surrealists sensed that nonrationality was the force animating twentieth-century Europe below the surface of traditional art, philosophy, and science. The surrealists celebrated the phenomena of their time, especially the products of technology, which expressed this underlying chaos. They conceived of an intensely concentrated truth beyond rationality—surreality—and committed themselves to attaining it.

Surrealism's immediate predecessor was Dada, and many surrealists were Dadaists first; but whereas Dada was negative in mood and principle, surrealism was positive. Surrealism involved an "almost programmatic . . . a surreal *conviction*" from which all art and behavior proceeded.[28] With energy, verve, and determination, the Surrealist movement formulated certain techniques for achieving surreality.

In order to achieve surreality, the surrealists cultivated their openness to the individual subconscious (through dreams, trances, madness) and to the universal laws of chance. Their art works were spontaneous, in theory at least; intellection had no part in creation. Also, the surrealist effort to compress time into another dimension was connected with the impulse toward the intensity of the creative experience.

28. Kauffmann, *Figures of Light*, p. 234.

The surrealists rejected traditional distinctions between life and art and between art genres, media, and values. Their art works are chaotic rather than structured traditionally. In particular, collages of visual images or of experiences of all sorts replaced conventional mimetic forms in all the arts. Surrealist principles have special affinity with expression through theater and cinema.

The surrealist artist and his audience together experienced surreality through the art work. Their relationship completed the impulse and intensified the moment.

René Clair, *Entr'acte*. Permission, Cinémathèque Française, Paris.

APPENDIX I

Plays, written by surrealists, referred to in the text, information on publication (in English translation, when available) and on first performance (if one took place).

N.B. *MFT* refers to Michael Benedikt and George E. Wellwarth, *Modern French Theatre*, E. P. Dutton and Company (New York, 1966).

Albert-Birot, Pierre — *Matoum and Tevibar (Matoum et Tévibar)*, 1916, play published in installments in Albert-Birot's periodical *SIC*, with poetic interludes contributed by Apollinaire, Reverdy, Soupault, Jacob.

Apollinaire, Guillaume — *The Breasts of Tiresias (Les Mamelles de Tirésias)*, in *MFT*. *The Breasts of Tiresias* was first performed June 24, 1917, at the Conservatoire René Maubel, under the author's direction.

Sky Blue (Couleur du Temps), 1917, in Apollinaire, *Oeuvres Poétiques* (Editions Gallimard, Paris, 1959). *Sky Blue* was first performed November 24, 1918, two weeks after the author's death, at the Conservatoire René Maubel.

Aragon, Louis — *The Mirror-Wardrobe One Fine Evening (L'Armoire à glace un beau soir)*, 1923, in *MFT*. *The Mirror-Wardrobe One Fine Evening* was first performed March 27, 1966, at the Grenier jaune.

Artaud, Antonin — Plays:
Jet of Blood (Jet du Sang), 1927, in *MFT*. *The Cenci (Les Cenci)*, 1935, in Artaud,

Oeuvres Complètes, Editions Gallimard, Paris, 1966. *The Cenci* was performed on May 6, 1935 at the Théâtre des Folies-Wagram. Artaud directed. This was the only Theater of Cruelty production.
Scenarios:
The Butcher's Revolt (La Révolte du Boucher), 1930.
18 Seconds, 1925.
The Shell and the Clergyman (La Coquille et le Clergyman), 1927, in *Tulane Drama Review* Vol. II, No. 1 ([T33], Fall 1966). *The Shell and the Clergyman,* filmed under the direction of Mme. Germaine Dulac, was shown on February 18, 1928 at the Ursulines Film Studio. Artaud was violently dissatisfied with this film version of his scenario and disrupted the showing.

Breton, André, and Soupault, Philippe

Please (S'il vous plaît), 1920, in *MFT*. *Please* was first performed March 27, 1920 during a soirée at the Théâtre de l'Oeuvre. The authors were among the actors.

Buñuel, Luis

Age of Gold (L'Age d'Or), filmed with some participation by Salvador Dali in 1930, first show shown at Studio 28 on October 28, 1930.
An Andalusian Dog (Un Chien Andalou), filmed with some participation by Salvador Dali in 1928, was first shown in 1928 at the Ursulines Film Studio.
Both scenarios appeared in single volume of Classic Film Script series (Simon and Schuster, New York, 1968).

Cocteau, Jean

The Wedding on the Eiffel Tower (Les Mariés de la Tour Eiffel), 1921, in *MFT*.

Daumal, René   *en gggarrrde,* 1924, in *MFT*.

Desnos, Robert   *La Place de L'Étoile* "anti-poem in nine scenes," 1914, in MFT. *La Place de L'Étoile* was first performed, with *The Breasts of Tiresias,* on April 20, 1949 at the Théâtre des Noctambules. Desnos wrote the play during the 1920s but continued to revise it until his death in a concentration camp.

Gilbert-Lecomte, Roger *The Odyssey of Ulysses the Palimped* (*L'Odyssée d'Ulysse le Palimpède*), 1924, in *MFT*.

Goll, Yvan   *Mathusalem ou l'Éternel Bourgeois,* 1919, in *L'Arche* (Paris, 1963). *Mathusalem* was first performed March 10, 1927 at the Théâtre Michel. Artaud appeared in the filmed portion.

Jarry, Alfred   *King Ubu* (*Ubu Roi*) in *MFT. King Ubu* was first performed on December 10, 1896 at Nouveau Theatre, Lugné Poë acted and directed; Toulouse-Lautrec, Pierre Bonnard and Jarry were among the designers of decor and masks. Jarry also wrote other plays about King Ubu: *Ubu Cuckolded* (*Ubu Cocu*), *Ubu Bound* (*Ubu Enchaîné*). Note that Jarry lived a generation earlier than the Surrealist movement.

Neveux, Georges   *Juliette or the Key to Dreams* (*Juliette ou la clé des songes*), 1930, France-Illustration-Le-Monde-Illustré (Paris, 1952). *Juliette or the Key to Dreams* first performed March 7, 1930 at the Théâtre de l'Avenue.

Pansaers, Clement   *The Smack-Smack on the Naked Negro's Ass* (*Le Pan-Pan au cul du Nu Nègre*),

1920 (Collection AIO Editions, Brussels, 1920).

Pansaers published *Bar Nicanor* the following year.

Picasso, Pablo

Desire Caught by the Tail (Le Désir Attrapé par la queue), 1944. *Desire Caught by the Tail* first performed in the salon of Michel Leiris. Participants included Albert Camus, Jean-Paul Sartre, Simone de Beauvoir.

Note that Picasso was never committed to the Surrealist movement.

Radiguet, Raymond

The Pelicans (Les Pélicans), 1921, in *MFT*.

Ribemont-Dessaignes, Georges

The Emperor of China (L'Empereur de Chine), 1925, in Ribemont-Dessaignes, *Théâtre* (Editions Gallimard, Paris, 1966). *The Emperor of China* was first performed December 5, 1925 at the Studio Art et Action.

Note that Ribemont-Dessaignes remained attached to Dada.

Rousseau, Henri (Le Douanier)

The Vengeance of a Russian Orphan Girl (La Vengeance d'une orpheline russe), 1899, *Paris-Théâtre*, No. 241, (Paris, 1967).

A Visit to the Exposition of 1899 (Une Visite à l'Exposition de 1899), 1899, (Pierre Cailler, Geneva, 1947).

Neither play was performed until the mid-1960s. Note that Rousseau lived a generation earlier than the surrealists, although in his old age he was a friend of Apollinaire's.

Roussel, Raymond

Impressions of Africa (Impressions d'Afrique), 1911, dramatized by the author from his novel and first performed on September 30, 1911 at the Théâtre Femina.

Note that Roussel was not part of the Surrealist movement.

Salacrou, Armand   *A Circus Story (L'Histoire du Cirque)*, 1922, in *MFT*.

Satie, Erik   *Medusa's Trap (Le Piège du Méduse)*, 1921. *Medusa's Trap* was first performed at the Théâtre Michel on May 24, 1921.

Tzara, Tristan   *Cloud Handkerchief (Mouchoir de Nuages)*, 1922 (Éditions de la Galerie Simon, Paris, 1925). *Cloud Handkerchief* was first performed on May 17, 1924 at the Théâtre de la Cigale. Among the participants were Marcel Herrand and Loie Fuller.

The Gas Heart (Le coeur à gaz), 1921, in *MFT*. *The Gas Heart* was first performed on June 10, 1921 at the Galerie Montaigne. The actors included Soupault, Aragon, Ribemont-Dessaignes, and Tzara himself. The performance on July 6, 1923 at the Théâtre Michel was the occasion of a brawl between Dada and the newly emergent surrealists.

The First Heavenly Adventure of Mr. Aspirin (La Première Aventure Céleste de M. Antipyrine), 1920, reproduced in part in Maguire (see Bibliography). *The First Heavenly Adventure of Mr. Aspirin* was first performed during a soirée on March 27, 1920 at the Théâtre de l'Oeuvre. The actors included: Breton, Soupault, Aragon, Éluard, Ribemont-Dessaignes, and Tzara himself.

Tzara wrote a sequel: *The Second . . .*
Note that Tzara remained the leader of Dada even after the surrealist defection.

Vitrac, Roger

Free Entry (Entrée Libre), 1922, in "Vitrac," *Théâtre*, Vol. III (Éditions Gallimard, Paris, 1964). The play had remained in the Fonds Doucet archives for forty years; this book contains the first English translation.

Médor and *The Painter (Le peintre)* in "Vitrac," *Théâtre*, Vol. III.

Victor, or Power to the Children (Victor ou les Enfants au pouvoir) in "Vitrac," *Théâtre*, Vol. II. *Victor* was first performed on December 24, 1928 at the Comédie des Champs-Elysées by the Théâtre Alfred-Jarry.

The Mysteries of Love (Les Mystères de l'Amour) in *MFT*.

The Mysteries of Love was first performed on June 1, 1927 at the Théâtre de Grenelle by the Théâtre Alfred-Jarry founded by Artaud, Robert Aron, and Vitrac himself.

Other information on Dada and surrealist productions in Béhar, *Étude sur le Théâtre Dada et Surréaliste* (see Bibliography).

APPENDIX II

Play in one act and seven scenes

Free Entry, unedited manuscript preserved in Fonds Doucet, signed and dated November 28, 1922.

The first three scenes and the last three are dreams; the fourth is the whole drama.

1st scene: Dream of Mr. Henry.
2nd scene: Dream of Mr. William Roze.
3rd scene: Dream of Mrs. Helen Roze.
5th scene: Dream of Mrs. Helen Roze.
6th scene: Dream of Mr. William Roze.
7th scene: Dream of Mr. Henry.

Mr. Henry takes the roles of the Man in Formal Dress, of Henry, of the Foundling Child, of the Sailor, and of Mr. Henry.

Mr. William Roze takes those of the Sheep, of William, of the Policeman, of the Bather, and of the Restaurant Manager.

Mrs. Helen Roze takes those of the Rare Bird, of the Prostitute, of the Newspaper Vendor, and of the Waitress.

One could, in each scene, indicate the face of the dreamer. One ought preferably to separate the scenes by blackouts.

(Author's note)

CHARACTERS

THE MAN IN FORMAL DRESS
THE RARE BIRD
THE SHEEP
WILLIAM

HENRY
THE PROSTITUTE
A WOMAN IN A TRAVELING OUTFIT (mute character)
MR. WILLIAM ROZE
MRS. HELEN ROZE
THE NEWSPAPER VENDOR (female)
THE POLICEMAN
THE FOUNDLING CHILD
THE BATHER
THE SAILOR
MR. HENRY
THE RESTAURANT MANAGER
THE WAITRESS

The scene takes place successively:
  In a forest
  By a lake
  In a street
  In a dining room
  In a public square
  By the sea
  and *In a restaurant*

SCENE I

(*A forest. Enter a* MAN IN FORMAL DRESS.)

MAN IN FORMAL DRESS. They invited me to dinner to strangle the children. Thanks a lot, that's not my dish. If that imbecile had not dressed up as a servant, I would still boast the excellence of a god so much the worse for my acquaintance. Woods of my childhood! It's odd the way one behaves nowadays. I left my boat on the other side of the lake but they've taught me to steal away. Hey there, this way, madame! The parapet at the end is carefully taken in every winter. I won't save you, the ice closes back over too quickly. Definitely my friend was wrong to get married. Hello Madame.

(*Enter the* RARE BIRD.)

THE RARE BIRD. Hello, William.

MAN IN FORMAL DRESS. She is deaf. (*Yelling.*) It is odd, madame, that you take me for the male parrot.

THE RARE BIRD. One thinks oneself in the middle of the belly. Myself, you know, William, I have aged a lot. When we were twenty, you had a horse which I never left. In the middle of the church I noticed that I was in my petticoat. No one paid attention to it, but you were red and you were saying: "It's the masons." They were all at the door with bludgeons and I recognized among them your best friend: Henry.

MAN IN FORMAL DRESS. Useless to insist. I do not want to be taken for a cad. You will manage with William. You recognized me quite well. Me, my name is Henry. Goodbye.

THE RARE BIRD. Well then! In that case, you ought to remove your moustache. No hard feelings. Come to dinner tomorrow.

MAN IN FORMAL DRESS. But what kind of bird can this be? Glasses in hand. . . . Glasses in hand. . . . Glasses in hand. The card hand passes. I've hit the jackpot.

SCENE II

(*By a lake.* THE SHEEP, *then* THE MAN IN FORMAL DRESS.)

THE SHEEP (*alone*). Helen, what a funny idea to have bought that fur-lined coat. From the service staircase of the gamekeeper's house the grass is all straight. The earth is subject to little explosions. I didn't forget my revolver, I even tried to fire at a tree. The gun jammed. Helen ran away. But she loves to run in the fields. All the more so since I had to avoid the notary who wouldn't stop casting his fishing rod.

(*Enter* THE MAN IN FORMAL DRESS.)

MAN IN FORMAL DRESS. His death?

SHEEP. You are in mourning, Henry!

MAN IN FORMAL DRESS. They entrusted to me a child of six. I lost him that night. He climbed the hotel staircase. My mother spoke to me in a low voice and took him away. You will not refuse me this, she said to me; she was so good to me that I gave her my engineer's diploma and a bird which I was very fond of. How is Helen?

SHEEP. We waited for you last night. You didn't come. We preferred not to have dinner. Besides, the roast was burned and the maid obstinately kept opening the door and bursting into laughter. I reprimanded her a bit harshly. She answered me: "Madame has Monsieur and that's that." She's a good girl.

MAN IN FORMAL DRESS. I certainly intend to come to dinner.

SHEEP. My wife went near the fire. She absolutely wanted a peignoir of cotton batting, and since she wanted it blue, she put it on right away. I begged her not to burn the letters without showing them to me. She gave me a terrible fright. The peignoir caught fire and she fainted. Her first words were: "If I can't do anything now, I'll change underwear every day, and we'll see."

MAN IN FORMAL DRESS. You imagine things.

SHEEP. I haven't decided yet. The last time we went shopping, Helen disappeared at every moment. The saleswomen astonished me by offering all sorts of objects: gloves, perfumes, razors, feathers, brushes. Luckily a policeman put an end to that comedy. He took me into a corner, and since I refused to show him my papers, he yelled in my ear: "But just look at yourself!" I realized that I was crying bitter tears. Helen nudged me with her elbow. She wanted to go home. I saw that she had changed stockings. I commented about it. She answered me: "It's the fashion now." Besides there wasn't anyone in the elevator.

MAN IN FORMAL DRESS. It's always like that on Friday.

SHEEP. I gladly excuse you, but you should take your hands out of your pockets.

MAN IN FORMAL DRESS (showing his hands). This? But these are pipes.

SHEEP. He's right, the beast. So much the better for you.

MAN IN FORMAL DRESS. Bah! I wear eyeglasses like everybody and I run faster than you. (He runs away.)   .

SHEEP. Robber! (He makes as if to run after him but mistakes the direction and throws himself in the water.)

SCENE III

(Paris, in a narrow street, at night.)

THE PROSTITUTE *(alone)*. It was a pretty room with flags on the walls. He had forced a blindfold over my eyes. He requested me to sit down and forgot me for a few instants. As he was turning around a table, I asked him what he had found. He returned with my mouth at his fingertips and put it back in place. He sat on my knees and unhooked my bodice behind my back. I remembered suddenly that my chemise was dirty. I begged him to let me alone. He did not insist and pointed out to me the odd design of his necktie. It was a green spiral where I don't know why the tick-tock of a watch could be heard. "Spain is not far," I thought. At that moment the door opened and a masked figure cried: "Morals squad." Immediately, undressed women sprang up from all the furniture. I followed them there.

(Enter WILLIAM.)

PROSTITUTE. Olives, olives, olives, olives.

WILLIAM. Have they harmed you?

PROSTITUTE. No sir. They advised me above all not to cross the street. This morning a child was run over. You see, there are still feathers in the mud.

WILLIAM. If you only knew what a hard time they're giving me.

PROSTITUTE. I haven't told you how their new apartment is arranged. There is an entrance with walls done in mirrors and bamboo. The living room connects with the kitchen which is also a bathroom. There is water on all the furniture and the bric-a-brac shelves are decorated with electric lamps. He was late in looking for the room which I didn't find.

I didn't dare ask them to open the back door. It was raining and I thought that you were waiting for me.

WILLIAM. No, I am coming back from my office. I was very busy. By the way, our friend Henry is dead.

PROSTITUTE. I know. It's the wicked women who killed him.

WILLIAM. You are better informed than I.

PROSTITUTE. Yes, aren't I? Aren't I? We, in our profession . . .
WILLIAM. So you don't want to? One hundred sous and the room?
PROSTITUTE. Swine! (*She bursts into sobs.*)

(*Enter* HENRY, *he is very pale. During the following dialogue, he speaks from a distance.*)

HENRY. You don't have to hold it against me.
PROSTITUTE. I don't hear you.
HENRY. First I thought of jumping out of the window, but on the balcony opposite was your rival who was waving to me. All of the inhabitants of the neighborhood had arranged to meet in front of the building to see me fall. One of them shouted: "Hands down." My valet reassured me. "It's the Protestants," he said. I found myself again in the middle of the boulevard where I learned, from a disheveled soldier, of your new profession.
PROSTITUTE. Well then! Mister Henry, we have ordered peach ice cream which you adore.
HENRY. That was a lot of trouble for nothing. I must leave on a trip.
PROSTITUTE. Far?
HENRY. That depends. Me, you know, I have something else to do.
PROSTITUTE. Business is business.

(*Enter a young woman enveloped in a traveling coat. She is carrying a valise.*)

HENRY. Don't kill her, she has no hands.

(THE PROSTITUTE *fires a revolver shot.*)

SCENE IV

(*A dining room.*)

(MRS. HELEN ROZE *is setting the table.* MR. WILLIAM ROZE *reads his newspaper.*)

HE. Everything all right?
SHE. Everything's all right.

HE. Your head?
SHE. I took a pill.
HE. Take another one.
SHE. The doorbell.
HE. No. It's the telephone in the courtyard.
SHE. I have a kind of feeling . . .
HE. Helen! Please.
SHE. You'll see.
HE. Certainly he will come.
SHE. Obviously.

(*Silence.*)

HE. Did you see?
SHE. No.
HE. They found a chronometer and a hat on the Pont des Arts.
SHE. Have they fished him out?
HE. No.

(*Silence.*)

HE. Pass me my pipe.
SHE. You're not going to smoke now.
HE. Yes I am.

(*The doorbell rings.*)

SHE. There, you see, it's not worth it. The doorbell.
HE. Pass me my pipe.
SHE. The doorbell.
HE. I tell you to pass me my pipe.

(*The doorbell rings.*)

SHE. Oh! I'm going to open the door.
HE. God Almighty.

(*Enter* MR. HENRY *who is leading* MRS. HELEN ROZE.)

MR. HENRY. Hello William, everything all right?
MR. WILLIAM ROZE. All right, and you?
MRS. HELEN ROZE. Now then, let's eat.

(*They sit down. Suddenly* MR. WILLIAM ROZE, *who has his back to the audience, overturns the table. The lamp breaks. The scene is plunged into darkness. Pursuit. Cries.*)

Don't kill her. William. William. William. Help. Murderer. Murderer. Murderer.

SCENE V

(*A public square.*)

NEWSPAPER VENDOR (female). (*She holds The* FOUNDLING CHILD *by the hand.*) Knives, scissors . . . knives, scissors . . . knives, scissors . . .

(ENTER THE POLICEMAN.)

NEWSPAPER VENDOR. It's me.

POLICEMAN. I ran away on a street which was transformed into a torrent. The passersby were crying: "He's burning, he's burning." But I had already put my uniform on and the automobile drivers who knew me greeted me grinning. They gave me a beautiful steel watch chain. Did you recognize me?

NEWSPAPER VENDOR. Oh! So many regiments pass by here.

POLICEMAN. I had to intervene in a matter where the examining magistrate didn't say a word without looking at me. Leaving his office he tapped my cheeks familiarly and said to me: "It's odd, isn't it?" I had slipped my left hand under my tunic, I couldn't get it back out again.

NEWSPAPER VENDOR. Have you read about the crime of Daunou Street?

POLICEMAN. Ah! It's you. Well, then! Follow me.

NEWSPAPER VENDOR. Officer, they dragged me by the hair and my head bounced back at every step of the staircase. They abandoned me in a prairie. It was hot. The grass was all red. The other one hardly cared about me. He let the doctor go ahead. "Let them put her on ice," he said. Me, I had advised him to leave me the little boy. But the child never wanted to go fetch that fur which I had had the time to hide under the sheets.

POLICEMAN. Is he yours, this little boy?

FOUNDLING CHILD. You're not going to take her away? She's bleeding.

POLICEMAN. What's your name?

FOUNDLING CHILD. Henry, Officer.

POLICEMAN. Ah . . . Henry, Henry, Henry, Henry . . .

(THE POLICEMAN *thrashes* THE NEWSPAPER VENDOR *and* THE FOUNDLING CHILD.)

SCENE VI

(*At the seashore. A beach cabana.*)

THE BATHER. The hotels of this country are chalk white. Someone wrote on the wall of my room: "225 days to go." But why do they let animals free in the corridors? There is always someone who puts his hand on your shoulder as you go out. In the garden there is a woman whom one never sees except from behind. I pursued her a whole day. She seems to be looking for somebody.

THE SAILOR. Have you come for the season?

BATHER. You seem to me to be suspicious, you!

SAILOR. You are white like linen, William.

BATHER. I danced all night. It seemed to me that they were preparing something in the room next door. Travelers went out with a lit candle, hand in front of the flame. I found out. They answered me, turning away their heads, "that it would all be over soon."

SAILOR. Do you want to see your wife again, William?

BATHER. Ah! . . . (*Indicating the cabana.*) I am sure that she is getting undressed in there. If you'd seen her, she had grown. She must be naked now.

(THE BATHER *moves toward the cabana.*)

SAILOR. Hey there! Where are you going, you?

BATHER. (*opening the door of the cabana*). Henry . . . look.

(*A woman cut into pieces is in the cabana.*)

SCENE VII

(A restaurant.)

MANAGER *(to* MR. HENRY, *who enters)*. Hello, Mr. Henry, what can I serve you?

MR. HENRY. Scallops in the shell.

MANAGER *(calling)*. It will be scallops in the shell for Mr. Henry.

MR. HENRY. Tell me, where did you find that dish?

(He indicates THE WAITRESS.*)*

WAITRESS. Ah!

(She drops a pile of plates.)

BIBLIOGRAPHY

(Sources and further references.)

Alexandrian, Sarane, *Surrealist Art*, trans. Gordon Clough (New York, Frederick A. Praeger, 1970).

Apollinaire, Guillaume, *Le Théâtre Italien* (Paris: Encyclopédie Littéraire Illustrée, 1910).

——, *Oeuvres Poétiques* (Paris: Éditions Gallimard, 1959).

Aragon, Louis, *Le Libertinage* (Paris: Éditions Gallimard, 1924).

Aristotle, *Poetics*, translated by S. H. Butcher (New York: Hill and Wang, 1921).

Artaud, Antonin, *À la grande nuit, ou le bluff surréaliste* (Paris: chez l'auteur, 1927).

——, *Oeuvres Complètes* (Paris: Éditions Gallimard, 1961–1966).

Auerbach, Erich, *Mimesis*, translated by Willard R. Trask (Princeton: Princeton University Press, 1953).

Balakian, Anna Elizabeth, *Literary Origins of Surrealism* (New York: Kings Crown Press, 1947).

——, *Surrealism: the Road to the Absolute* (New York: The Noonday Press, 1959).

Bédouin, Jean Louis, *Vingt Ans de Surréalisme* (Paris: Éditions Denoël, 1961).

Béhar, Henri, *Étude sur le Théâtre Dada et Surréaliste* (Paris: Editions Gallimard, 1967).

——, "La Question du Théâtre Surréaliste, ou le Théâtre en Question," *Europe*, No. 475–476, Paris, (Nov.–Dec. 1968), p. 164.

——, *Roger Vitrac* (Paris: A. G. Nizet, 1966).

Bergson, Henri, *An Introduction to Metaphysics* (London: The Macmillan Company, 1921).

——, "Laughter," in *Comedy*, edited and translated by Wylie Sypher (New York: Doubleday & Company, Inc., Garden City, 1956).

Breton, André, *First Papers of Surrealism: "hanging by André*

Breton"/his twine Marcel Duchamp (New York: Coordinating Council of French Relief Societies, Inc., 1947).

————, Manifestes du Surréalisme (Paris: Jean-Jacques Pauvert, 1962).

Brustein, Robert, The Theater of Revolt (Boston and Toronto: Little, Brown and Company, 1964).

Cage, John, Silence: Lectures and Writings (New York: Wesleyan University Press, 1961).

Clancier, Georges-Emmanuel, Rimbaud au Surréalisme (Paris: Éditions Pierre Seghers, 1959).

Clapham, John, The Economic Development of France and Germany 1815–1914 (New York: The Macmillan Company, 1923).

Cocteau, Jean, Poésie Critique (Paris: Éditions Gallimard, 1959).

Corvin, Michel, Le Théâtre Nouveau en France (Paris: Presses Universitaires de France, 1969).

Debresse, René (ed.), Testament d'Apollinaire (Paris: René Guy Cadou, 1945).

Delpit, Louise, Paris-Théâtre (Northampton, Mass. and Paris: Departments of Modern Languages of Smith College, Vol. VI, Nos. 1 and 2; Oct. 1924–Jan. 1925).

Dreier, Katherine S. and Matta Echaurren, Duchamp's Glass: An Analytical Reflection (New York: Société Anonyme Inc., Museum of Modern Art, 1944).

Duchamp, Marcel, Marchand du Sel (Paris: Le Terrain Vague, 1958).

Encore, No. 51, Sept.–Oct. 1964, Vol. II, No. 5, New York.

————, No. 54, Mar.–Apr. 1965, Vol. 12, No. 2, New York.

Esslin, Martin, The Theater of the Absurd (Garden City, New York: Doubleday & Company, Inc., 1961).

Fergusson, Francis, The Idea of a Theater (Garden City, New York: Doubleday & Company, Inc., 1953).

Fowlie, Wallace, Dionysius in Paris (New York: Meridian Books, Inc., 1960).

Freud, Sigmund, The Interpretation of Dreams, translated by James Strachey (New York: Avon Books, 1966).

————, Civilization and its Discontents, edited and translated by James Strachey (New York: W. W. Norton & Company, Inc., 1961).

Gilman, Richard, The New Republic, New York, November 9, 1968.

Goll, Yvan, *Yvan Goll: Poètes d'aujourd'hui* (Belgiques: Éditions Pierre Seghers, 1956).

Grotowski, Jerzy, *Towards a Poor Theatre* (New York: Simon and Schuster, 1969).

Hadas, Moses, *Introduction to Classical Drama* (New York: Bantam Books, 1966).

Hamel, Frank, "Art in Advertisement," in *Colour* (London: 1916).

Hiatt, Charles, *Picture Posters* (London: George Bell and Sons, 1895).

Hughes, H. Stuart, *Consciousness and Society* (New York: Vintage Books, 1958).

Hugnet, Georges, *L'Aventure Dada* (Paris: Éditions Seghers, 1971).

Jarry, Alfred, *Selected Works of Alfred Jarry*, edited by Roger Shattuck and Simon Watson Taylor (New York: Grove Press, Inc., 1965).

Kauffmann, Stanley, *Figures of Light* (New York: Harper and Row, 1971).

Kirby, Michael, *Happenings* (New York: E. P. Dutton and Co., Inc., 1964).

Knapp, Bettina L., *Antonin Artaud* (New York: David Lewis, 1969).

Kyrou, Aldo, *Le Surréalisme au Cinéma* (Paris: Le Terrain Vague, 1963).

Lautréamont, Le Comte de (Isidore Lucien Ducasse), *Les Chants de Maldoror* (Brussels: Paris et Bruxelles, 1874).

Lebel, Robert, *Marcel Duchamp* (Paris: Éditions Trianon, 1959).

Lemaître, Georges, *From Cubism to Surrealism* (Cambridge, Mass.: Harvard University Press, 1941).

L'Oeuvre, Revue Internationale des Arts du Théâtre (Paris: Éditions Albert Morance, 1924–1925).

Le Surréalisme au Service de la Révolution (Paris: 1933).

Longinus, Dionysius Cassius, *'Longinus': On Sublimity*, translated by D. A. Russell (Oxford: Clarendon Press, 1965).

Maguire, Robert, *"Le Hors Théâtre," Essai sur la signification du théâtre de notre temps;* Typescript text in the Sorbonne Library (Paris, 1963).

Mallarmé, Stéphane, *Oeuvres Complètes de Stéphane Mallarmé* (Paris: Bibliothèque de la Pléiade, Librairie Gallimard, 1956).

Matthews, J. H., *An Introduction to Surrealism* (Pennsylvania: Pennsylvania State University Press, 1965).

Nacenta, Raymond, *Le surréalisme: sources—histoire—affinités* (Paris: Galerie Charpentier, MCMLXIV).

Nadeau, Maurice, *The History of Surrealism*, translated by Richard Howard (New York: The Macmillan Company, 1966).

Nin, Anaïs, *The Diary of Anaïs Nin* (New York: Swallow Press, 1966).

Peacock, Ronald, *The Art of Drama* (London: Routledge and Kegan Paul, Ltd., 1957).

Poncetton, François, "La Tour Eiffel a cinquante ans I," in *La Revue universelle*, Tome LXXVII, No. 6, Paris, June 15, 1939.

————, "La Tour Eiffel a cinquante ans II," in *La Revue universelle*, Tome LXXVIII, No. 7, Paris, July 1, 1939.

Prévost, Jean, *Eiffel* (Paris: Les Éditions Rieder, 1929).

Pronko, Leonard Cabell, *Avant-Garde: The Experimental Theater in France* (Berkeley and Los Angeles: University of California Press, 1964).

Raymond, Marcel, *From Baudelaire to Surrealism* (New York: Wittenborn, Schultz, Inc., 1950).

Read, Herbert, *Art and Society* (New York: Schocken Books, 1966).

Richter, Hans, *Dada: Art and Anti-Art* (West Germany: McGraw-Hill Book Company, n.d.).

Rivière, Henri, *Les Trente-Six vues de la Tour Eiffel* (Paris: Imprimerie Eugène Verneau, 1902).

Roussel, Raymond, *Impressions of Africa* translated by Lindy Foord and Reyner Heppenstall (London: Calder and Boyars, 1966).

Rubin, William S., *Dada, Surrealism, and Their Heritage* (New York: The Museum of Modern Art, 1968).

Sellin, Eric, *The Dramatic Concepts of Antonin Artaud* (Chicago: The University of Chicago Press, 1968).

Serreau, Geneviève, *Histoire du nouveau théâtre* (Paris: Éditions Gallimard, 1966).

Sewell, Elizabeth, *The Field of Nonsense* (London: Chatto and Windus, 1952).

Shattuck, Roger, *The Banquet Years* (New York: Vintage Books, Random House, 1968).

SIC, Paris, 1916–1919.

Sokel, Walter, *The Writer in Extremis* (Stanford, California: Stanford University Press, 1959).

Sontag, Susan, *Against Interpretation* (New York: Dell Publishing Co., Inc., 1967).

Sylvester, David, *René Magritte* (New York: Frederick A. Praeger, Inc., 1969).

Tomkins, Calvin, *The Bride and the Bachelors: Five Masters of the Avant-Garde* (New York: The Viking Press, Inc., 1968).

Tulane Drama Review, Winter 1963; Vol. 8, No. 2.

————, Fall 1966, Vol. 11, No. 1.

Tzara, Tristan, *Lampisteries, précédées de sept manifestes Dada* (Paris: chez Jean-Jacques Pauvert, 1963).

————, *Picasso et les chemins de la connaissance* (Geneva: éditions d'art Albert Skira, n.d.).

Vaché, Jacques, *Lettres de la Guerre* (Paris: Au Sans Pareil, 1919).

Veinstein, André, *Du Théâtre Libre au Théâtre Louis Jouvet: Les Théâtres d'art à travers leur périodiques* (Paris: Éditions Billandot, 1955).

View, New York, Vol. I, Nos. 7–8; Oct.–Nov., 1941.

————, New York, Vol. II, March, 1942.

————, New York, Vol. V, March, 1945.

XXᵉ siècle; Nouvelle série, No. 3, June, 1952.

Vitrac, Roger, *Humoristiques* (Paris: Éditions de la Nouvelle Revue Française, 1927).

Waldberg, Patrick, *Max Ernst peintures pour Paul Éluard* (Paris: Editions Denoël, 1969).

INDEX